Advance praise for
DEEPAK CHOPRA'S *AWAKENING*

"*Awakening* is possible, and Deepak Chopra's guidebook helps us achieve it."

—CHRISTOF KOCH, PH.D., NEUROSCIENTIST;
AUTHOR OF *Then I Am Myself the World*

"Deepak Chopra has given us a guide to wake up to who we truly are. *Awakening* is powerful, practical, and life-changing—it shows us how to move beyond fear and step into freedom, purpose, and possibility."

—JAY SHETTY, #1 *New York Times* BESTSELLING AUTHOR;
HOST OF THE *On Purpose* PODCAST; FORMER MONK

"Deepak Chopra has given us a book of rare depth and practicality. *Awakening* reminds us that success and well-being are measured not by external achievements but by the peace and awareness we cultivate each day. With clarity and wisdom, Chopra offers us a timeless guide to living more fully—more present, more connected, and more awake to the possibilities of life."

—ARIANNA HUFFINGTON, FOUNDER AND CEO OF
THRIVE GLOBAL AND AUTHOR OF *The Sleep Revolution*

"Who am I? Why do I act as I do? Am I making the best use of my time on earth? As I've grown older, I've become increasingly intent on discovering the truth about myself. In *Awakening*, **Deepak Chopra renews ancient Vedic traditions, offering a contemporary path to enlightenment. In this highly readable book, he both challenges and guides us toward a deeper self-awareness—an incomparable reward in itself.**"

—LEONARD MLODINOW, *New York Times* BESTSELLING
AUTHOR OF *Emotional: How Feelings Shape Our Thinking* AND
The Grand Design (WITH STEPHEN HAWKING)

"Spacetime is a headset. My body is an avatar in a spacetime VR. I may think I am my body and must perish with it. But I create this headset and countless others. **Deepak Chopra expertly and compassionately guides us in awakening to our true nature and creative power** beyond our spacetime headset."

—DONALD HOFFMAN, PROFESSOR OF COGNITIVE SCIENCES, UNIVERSITY OF CALIFORNIA, IRVINE; AUTHOR OF *The Case Against Reality*

"Deepak Chopra's *Awakening* is totally compelling. It radiates the liberating wisdom of Buddha, Jesus, Blake, and Rumi—expressed in Chopra's own unique, present, and timeless way. I love how it arrives as a perfectly timed manifesto for the difficult moment we are all facing. This book is a must-read and a true companion for our journey, helping us relax into awakening and discover the beauty, peace, and joy that are our human birthright."

—ROBERT THURMAN, COLUMBIA UNIVERSITY,
BUDDHIST STUDIES PROFESSOR EMERITUS; CO-AUTHOR OF
Man of Peace: The Illustrated Life Story of the Dalai Lama of Tibet

"Grounded in many decades of Deepak Chopra's own visionary and spiritual path, *Awakening* is perhaps his most timely, transformative, and practical invitation and guide to remembering and embodying the whole-being of who we really are."

—JUDE CURRIVAN, COSMOLOGIST AND AUTHOR;
CO-FOUNDER OF WHOLEWORLD-VIEW

"In *Awakening*, Deepak Chopra distills a lifetime of study, practice, and reflection into a work of luminous simplicity and depth. His words arise from the authority of direct experience and carry the quiet power to return us to the source of our own being. Each page is both a doorway and an invitation into the living presence of awareness itself—the ground of freedom, love, and peace. This book is a true companion for anyone drawn to the essence of the spiritual path."

—RUPERT SPIRA, AUTHOR OF *The Nature of Consciousness;*
Being Aware of Being Aware; AND *The Shining of Being*

"Deepak Chopra's new book, *Awakening*, goes to places where few can accompany him—places of new openings, new opportunities, and, most important, paths to an awakened presence, our true eternal Presence. *Awakening* **pushes us to the awakened persons we truly are, beings full of wisdom and awareness. All within reach, here and there.**"

—MENAS KAFATOS, *New York Times* BESTSELLING AUTHOR;
FLETCHER JONES ENDOWED PROFESSOR OF
COMPUTATIONAL PHYSICS, CHAPMAN UNIVERSITY

"I have always believed that conscious living is the key to a better, kinder world. Chopra's words in *Awakening* do just that, helping us to find clarity, wisdom, and happiness."

—DIANE VON FURSTENBERG,
FASHION DESIGNER AND PHILANTHROPIST

"In *Awakening,* Deepak Chopra expands on his classic teachings with his greatest clarity, directness, and kindness yet—pointing the way to enlightenment for seekers everywhere."

—NEIL THEISE, M.D., PROFESSOR OF PATHOLOGY,
NEW YORK UNIVERSITY SCHOOL OF MEDICINE

"Dr. Deepak Chopra offers us a beautiful and highly accessible way to bring presence to every experience, so that we may live a fulfilling and meaningful life where anxiety and fear are replaced with clarity and joy."

—RUDOLPH E. TANZI, PHD, DIRECTOR, MCCANCE CENTER
FOR BRAIN HEALTH; DIRECTOR, GENETICS AND AGING
RESEARCH UNIT, MASS GENERAL BRIGHAM;
JOSEPH P. AND ROSE F. KENNEDY PROFESSOR
OF NEUROLOGY, HARVARD MEDICAL SCHOOL

"*Awakening* masterfully guides readers on a transformative journey from the conditioned mind to the essence of fundamental reality. Dr. Deepak Chopra, a distinguished alumnus of the All India Institute of Medical Sciences (AIIMS), New Delhi, **illuminates the path to wholeness, where healing, health, and self-regulation converge through the power of homeostasis. This book is a profound invitation to rediscover inner balance and embrace true well-being."**

—PROFESSOR M. SRINIVAS, DIRECTOR, AIIMS, NEW DELHI

"In *Awakening,* Deepak Chopra offers a luminous road map to living with greater clarity, freedom, and purpose. Through timeless sutras and modern insights, he shows how awakening is not a distant ideal but a natural possibility available to everyone. This book is a transformative companion for anyone ready to embrace their full potential."

—ROBERT WALDINGER, PSYCHIATRIST; DIRECTOR OF
THE HARVARD STUDY OF ADULT DEVELOPMENT

"*Awakening* is the call we need to wake up from the nightmare of artificial, even if inadvertent, self-destruction. With this book, the path to natural, self-created evolution is open."

—ERVIN LASZLO, PHILOSOPHER OF SCIENCE;
AUTHOR OF *Science and the Akashic Field*

"When Werner Heisenberg let go of his mental conceptualizing, he was able to become aware of Nature's message in the form of quantum physics, which speaks of a domain beyond the spacetime theater—'a hidden reality that cannot be penetrated by the five senses,' to quote Deepak Chopra's phrase describing the awakened perception of reality. Heisenberg probably didn't see himself as being on a spiritual path, but his choice to become awake to Nature placed him on a path that ultimately unites with the age-old insights of sages. Physics as a spiritual path? Einstein certainly thought so, as did Newton. Physics is just one path, but a potent one if we can hear its message to relinquish our voluntary confinement to the limiting cage that we call 'spacetime' and to recognize awareness as ubiquitous—in ourselves and in everything in our world. **Chopra invites us to become aware in our own way, based on a generous offering of the timeless wisdom of those who have awakened before us.**"

—RUTH E. KASTNER, PHD; AUTHOR OF *Adventures in Quantumland*

"Chopra's sutras are both clear and profound, and through them he generously transmits the insights of the great Indian seers and the wisdom of the world's spiritual traditions. This book is the mature quintessence of his teaching that awakening is a possibility for everyone."

—RUPERT SHELDRAKE, BIOLOGIST; AUTHOR OF MORE THAN
ONE HUNDRED SCIENTIFIC PAPERS; KNOWN FOR WORK
ON MORPHIC RESONANCE AND SPIRITUAL QUESTIONS

"Can mere mortals escape the cave? Is enlightenment possible? I've always had doubts. But Deepak Chopra's warm, wonderful new book, *Awakening*, makes me want to give it a shot."

—JOHN HORGAN, SCIENCE JOURNALIST; AUTHOR
OF *The End of Science* AND *Rational Mysticism*

"*Awakening* serves as a profound act of public service, akin to the mission of India's Public Service Broadcaster, Doordarshan. Through its soulful and insightful narrative, **Dr. Deepak Chopra offers transformative wisdom that inspires a deeper connection to wholeness and well-being. This book shines as a guiding light for those seeking meaningful personal growth.**"

—BRIJ BAKSHI, FORMER DIRECTOR, DOORDARSHAN

"*Awakening* reminds us that true freedom begins within. Deepak Chopra offers a vision of life beyond fear—one where awareness, intuition, and boundless potential become our daily reality."

"As I read the sutras in Deepak Chopra's *Awakening*, it felt like someone was gently leading me back to my own source. Every page has a clarity that clears up confusion and a simplicity that speaks to the heart. The thing that moved me the most was that the book doesn't just talk about awakening; it makes it seem possible, natural, and even inevitable. I often stopped, not to think more, but to be more. These sutras aren't just ideas; they are real truths that lead us to freedom, wholeness, and the infinite present moment. I will read this book over and over, and each time I do, I will find something new that resonates with me."

"Deepak Chopra's call for our awakening of awareness is very timely and should be heard. I highly recommend this book."

BY DEEPAK CHOPRA

AWAKENING

AWAKENING

·

THE PATH TO FREEDOM
AND ENLIGHTENMENT

DEEPAK CHOPRA, MD

HARMONY

NEW YORK

HARMONY BOOKS
An imprint of Random House
A division of Penguin Random House LLC
1745 Broadway, New York, NY 10019
HarmonyBooks.com | RandomHouseBooks.com
penguinrandomhouse.com

Hardcover ISBN 978-0-593-23605-5
Ebook ISBN 978-0-593-23606-2
International edition ISBN 978-0-593-98108-5

Printed in the United States of America on acid-free paper

1st Printing

FIRST EDITION

BOOK TEAM: PRODUCTION EDITOR: *Mark Birkey* •
MANAGING EDITOR: *Allie Fox* • PRODUCTION MANAGER: *Mark Maguire* •
COPY EDITOR: *Diana Drew* • PROOFREADERS: *Pam Feinstein, Judy Kiviat, Russell Powers, Alissa Fitzgerald* • INDEXER: *Ina Gravitz*

Title page art from adobestock/serkorkin

Book design by Barbara M. Bachman

The authorized representative in the EU for product safety and compliance is Penguin Random House Ireland, Morrison Chambers, 32 Nassau Street, Dublin D02 YH68, Ireland. https://eu-contact.penguin.ie.

TO THE CARETAKERS

OF WISDOM

Contents

•

Introduction

Invitation to a New Life

A NEW WAY OF LIFE—THE AWAKENED LIFE—OPENS UP WITH a single decision: to know the truth about reality, including the truth about yourself. To be awake is to be fully conscious about what is real and what isn't. Every step along the way brings a greater sense of lightness and freedom. Nothing feels freer than being yourself, as most people realize when they reach a point when simply being here is enough. But mostly it isn't enough. Everyone is preoccupied with an unending stream of desires, duties, and demands. We are so accustomed to this existence that being told to wake up is hard to fathom, or outright impossible.

What keeps us in thrall is a waking dream that is collectively shared with everyone else. Without the strangely surreal happenings in the dreams we have when we're asleep, the waking dream is totally convincing and crystal clear. Once you stretch your arms in the morning after a night's sleep, you automatically enter the waking dream with no thought that you need to wake up twice.

This second awakening is so important that in the Indian spiritual tradition it is called a "second birth." Clarity dawns about who you really are, where you come from, and why you are here. Modern people struggle with all these issues. Even if you don't give a thought to India or any spiritual tradition—East or West—a deep intuition motivates anyone who heeds it; that life can't be as mundane, conflicted, fearful, difficult, and full of pain as the life we have accepted without question.

The awakened life has always been an alternative. Its promise is renewed with every generation. The present generation, particularly in the West, has set up its own standards of proof. Awakening must be described in ordinary language, rationally laid out, presented with convincing logic, and, above all, suited to solving the array of problems—both personal and global—that afflict our troubled times. For the vast majority of people, reverence for ancient traditions doesn't enter the picture.

Nodding to those demands, the following pages provide a guide to the awakened life that anyone can follow. There is nothing the reader needs in the way of faith or belief. The argument for awakening is couched in straight talk without offering either a carrot or a stick. The truth must be convincing on its own. Only then can you make a choice about whether or not to open the door to a new life.

I'll ask for only one article of trust. Trust that awakening is natural. All creatures and plants survive because they follow their own nature, without deviation or doubts. A predatory wolf or lion isn't weighed down by its history of past decisions or pining over lost love. There is no reason for *Homo sapiens* to be excluded from this scheme. We have evolved beyond it. As the most privileged life-form on Earth, we are free to make choices, including the choice to wake up. In awakening, we are liberated from the nightmare of our personal and collective suffering, by the natural process of reconnecting with our true nature. We are designed to wake up, which will reveal who we really are.

At the same time, we relinquish the separate, isolated self. This isn't a sacrifice but an immense gain. Seen clearly, human beings are an expression of pure consciousness, which is the boundless, infinite source at the root of existence.

If I had to describe my entire career in a single phrase, it would come down to *awakening as a possibility for everyone*. Awakening isn't reserved for a select group of sages, saints, visionaries, and poets, inspiring as they are. By its nature, human awareness expands. Yours has been expanding since birth, and if you don't feel aware all the time, the pattern of stressful modern life is chiefly to blame.

Awareness cannot be destroyed; it is the basis of having a mind in the first place. But most people are distracted by the constant activity of the mind as it thinks, feels, and senses experiences. Screened behind this activity, your awareness goes unnoticed because it has no voice and doesn't attract attention to itself.

Nevertheless, your state of awareness determines in huge measure how your life will turn out and how your everyday existence is proceeding here and now. A major revelation in the awakened life is that existence *is* conscious. There is nothing in creation without some degree of awareness. This revelation deposes human beings as the only creatures who possess consciousness. The long journey begun by our hominid ancestors did not start from a blank slate of unconsciousness. Certainly a journey occurred from origins over millions of years, but consciousness guided our evolutionary ascent.

If this proposition overturns the apple cart, it is only one of the realizations that arrive spontaneously when someone awakens in consciousness. For the moment, set this aside. The practical challenge I faced when conceiving this book was how to give readers an experience of pure consciousness as the fundamental source of their lives. You can't think yourself awake, and no one can talk you into it.

After pondering this question, I decided that nothing would do but the truth. Give the reader the most profound truths about consciousness and trust that, in the end, the truth will win out. In one sense this is like presenting evidence in court that piles up until guilt or innocence becomes undeniable. In another sense, I'm giving a secular version of Jesus's teaching, "Know the truth, and the truth shall set you free."

At its most profound, the path to the truth was meticulously laid out in the Vedic tradition thousands of years ago in India through Gyan Yoga. The purpose of the eight branches, or "limbs," of Yoga is to unite a person with pure consciousness. *Gyan* in Sanskrit refers to knowledge or wisdom. So this is the path of wisdom to achieve a high state of consciousness.

Although my daily routine includes several other limbs of Yoga, among them the postures of Hatha Yoga taught in yoga classes, what comes naturally to me is Gyan Yoga. I thirst for knowledge, read voraciously, revere ancient texts, and feel great inspiration whenever I discover an expression of wisdom. I am going to do my best in these chapters to forge a bond with you, the reader, based on a similar thrill of discovery.

Although *Gyan* means both knowledge and wisdom, I want to distinguish between the two. *Knowledge* is generally the word we choose when speaking about external facts and information. You get a college degree based on the field of knowledge you major in. *Wisdom* is interior; it comes in the form of insight, realizing the truth behind the knowledge your mind acquires.

In the modern secular world, wisdom has become suspect, largely because skeptics apply the wrong tests to it. They judge wisdom by the same standards used to validate fingerprints or to measure the molecular weight of plutonium—tests suited for objective facts, but not for subjective insight.

An insight has no molecular weight and leaves no fingerprints behind. Deciding that wisdom is unreliable, like other subjective experiences, is a perfect example of asking the wrong question to begin with. Wisdom is truth gained through inner discoveries in consciousness. I always compare the ancient seers, or rishis, of Vedic India to Einsteins of consciousness. Einstein unveiled the hidden principles governing the physical universe; the rishis uncovered the inner path to pure consciousness, which is just as universal. The legacy they left behind constitutes Gyan Yoga. It reveals a hidden dimension of life that is more real than the physical world because Gyan Yoga can explain the physical world, while science cannot explain consciousness.

It is fascinating to discover that truths revealed in the ancient past pertain to your life today. Pure consciousness embraces everyone. This makes the possibility of the awakened life open to everyone.

To reach the state of awakening, you need access to the deeper truth of who you are and what life is all about. I've chosen the most authentic written form that Gyan Yoga takes—the axioms known in Sanskrit as sutras. There are thirty-three sutras here, modified for modern understanding. Each presents one angle of wisdom in concentrated form, followed by a practical section that addresses how to find your own personal wisdom. The infinite potential that is the essence of being human can't be realized in the written word—only the experience of insight is ultimately valid. But for millennia the sutra has come closer to expressing the truth than any other form. The exalted role of wisdom needs to be revived in our time, which is dominated by external knowledge. If wisdom can be resurrected, untold horizons lie ahead and, more immediately, the urgent global problems facing us can be solved at the source.

THE PATH OF AWAKENING

1.

The
Eternal Promise

•

AS A CHILD, I GREW UP IN A FAMILY THAT WAS ECUMENICAL TO a fault. At one extreme was my religious mother, who went to temple in New Delhi every morning for her devotions. At the other extreme was my father, a Western-trained doctor who went to his cardiology practice every morning and whose only religion was science. For some reason, this contradiction didn't confuse me. Our house was open to people of all faiths, of which India has more than any other country. Some people came to sing hymns to the music of a harmonium in the living room; others gathered outside for a free medical consultation— my father turned no one away for being poor.

Such openness of heart made an indelible impression on me. I didn't realize, as I matured and followed in my father's footsteps, that my mother stood for something I now know as *the eternal promise*. It is the promise of full awakening to who we really are. And who are we? We are the expression of pure, infinite, unbounded awareness. To a religious person like my mother, awakening reveals the divine presence in everything. A rationalist like my father might have accepted what the physicist Freeman Dyson once wrote: "God is what mind becomes when it passes the threshold of our comprehension."

Without awakening, no one can reach the full potential of being human. In fact, it becomes impossible to know why we are here in the first place. Only as expressions of unbounded awareness do we find a timeless footing and a place in the cosmos.

The eternal promise is open to everyone without their conscious awareness. If the promise could speak, we'd hear a voice in our heads whispering, "Don't you want to wake up?" But the voice is silent. Hardly anyone, just the smallest sliver of humanity, gets the message. Therefore, the eternal promise goes unfulfilled.

If we don't hear the message, how do we even know that awakening exists? There are clues, beginning with the words of those who have awakened.

"If the doors of perception were cleansed, everything would appear to man as it is: Infinite." (William Blake)

"When you do things from your soul, you feel a river moving in you, a joy." (Rumi)

"I wish I could show you, when you are lonely or in darkness, the astonishing light of your own being." (Hafiz)

Blake, Rumi, and Hafiz are often described as mystical poets, but they are more accurately called awakened poets. Their words reflect the profound truths that awareness revealed to them. Awakening is not merely a poetic or mystical concept; it has real, tangible effects on a person's life. Those who wake up often describe a profound sense of well-being that touches every aspect of life—mentally, emotionally, physically, and spiritually. This deep connection between awareness and well-being has been observed for centuries, but today we can actually measure it. Later in this book, we'll explore a framework for assessing this transformation, helping you understand where you are on the path to awakening.

When people first encounter the idea of awakening, they often find it mystifying. And being mystified keeps them from diving any deeper. Yet the process of waking up is natural, and the path is not difficult. In fact, a small percentage of people awaken spontaneously. Looking back, they can pinpoint the exact day it happened, though why they were chosen remains a mystery no one can explain.

A HIDDEN CHOICE

The opposite of waking up is being asleep, not physically but by living unconscious of your true nature, hidden behind everyday existence. To be awake is to break out of the limited state of awareness that each of us occupies.

Sheer inertia makes today feel much like yesterday. We are immersed in a reality where waking up isn't a choice, practically speaking, because we fall back in every situation on a host of behaviors that screen "real" reality. Pause to consider how the following list applies to you, not with an attitude of self-judgment but by taking an honest look in the mirror.

HOW MUCH ARE YOU INFLUENCED?

Routine: a pattern of familiar default activity during the day
Habit: automatic behavior that runs on its own inertia, even when you want to change
Old conditioning: secondhand responses you picked up during childhood from your family
Stubborn beliefs: ingrained opinions you accept without examining them
Groupthink: things you say and do to conform with society
Ego needs: the priorities you set that look out for number one
Desire: the force behind wanting, craving, envy, and jealousy
External demands and duties: the things you do for money or to satisfy other people
Personal fears and insecurity: the things that keep you up at night

The list could be much longer because even the most routine, boring, unfulfilled, and thwarted life is complex. It is impossible to get to the bottom of every cause and influence that shaped you. But we don't have to dive into the murky subconscious or the dimly remembered past for answers. If you can identify with the experience of being hemmed in, frustrated, and limited, you are ready to wake up.

Here we encounter the divide between waking up and the rest of life, which is all about doing, thinking, feeling, talking, and the like.

That dimension is rooted in the thinking mind. Awakening, by contrast, is rooted in awareness. This difference turns out to be the key because the two worlds of "in here" and "out there" aren't separate but intimately linked. There is no such thing as an experience without awareness, which makes it more fundamental than thinking, feeling, and doing.

If you pay attention to your state of awareness, nothing else is needed to wake up. For all practical purposes, your self-awareness is the inner space where waking up occurs. It helps to refer to those few people who wake up spontaneously. What they experience contains the following elements.

THE EXPERIENCES OF AWAKENED PEOPLE

They have fewer thoughts, mostly those involving practical matters.

There is an absence of anxiety.

They feel present in the moment, not overshadowed by the past.

They face the unknown with openness and a lack of assumptions.

Their sense of "I" feels expanded.

They experience bliss in some form.

They don't feel trapped inside the limitations of the physical body. They may experience a sense of physical lightness or expansiveness.

Their five senses are more alert.

Their existence feels free.

YOU ARE MORE READY THAN YOU THINK

Some people are more self-aware than others—psychologists consider this a mark of maturing into adulthood—but everyone has a self and everyone is aware. The fact that you answer to your name is a sign of self-awareness developed before you could walk. Awakening takes this essential human trait and carries it to its fullest extent. Since spontaneous awakening is so rare, for the rest of us there is a path. After decades of experience, I've come to the conclusion that the discipline of meditation over years and decades is beyond all but a few people. Meditation has a practical value for everyone, however, as a pure experience of silent awareness. The experience is simple but necessary. If you haven't meditated before, here's an exercise for contacting pure awareness.

Finding Simple Awareness

EXERCISE

Choose a moment when you feel calm and undistracted. Choose a space, preferably dimly lit, where you won't be interrupted.

Sit quietly with your eyes closed and take a few deep breaths or sighs to settle yourself.

As you breathe, have the sensation of descending into the heart region at the center of your chest.

When you feel centered and calm, do nothing more. Just experience the sensation. Without effort, you will notice that thoughts come and go. They rise from silence and fall back again. Pay attention to the difference between thinking and not-thinking.

Not-thinking is simple awareness.

VERY FEW PEOPLE HAVE found simple awareness on their own, but a few repetitions of this exercise will make the experience clear. The state of simple awareness is the launching place for all higher states of consciousness, including awakening. Awakening is established when the thinking mind is no longer your default. Instead, the state of not-thinking is your new default.

What makes simple awareness so effective is that it is effortless and always accessible. The discipline of a lifetime of meditation or mindfulness practices isn't required. You are in the state of simple awareness anytime something interests you. Your attention focuses on that thing—a movie, a hobby, a news report, a deep conversation, and so on—without much notice, because the object of interest is outside yourself. Paying attention to the world "out there" preoccupies everyone already. You have to get the knack of paying attention "in here," making awareness your focus.

I speak of a knack because the territory "in here" is full of objects just like those in the external world, an endless stream of thoughts, feelings, sensations, images, and memories. When they draw your attention, you aren't noticing awareness by itself. It is always attached to an object. But you have had lots of experience being in simple awareness, so noticing it requires no great leap, just a small shift of focus.

It's helpful to be guided by the experiences of people who are awakened because, for them, being aware of awareness is their default. They can't avoid being aware, which is the same as saying that they don't lapse into the unconscious state of routine, habit, old conditioning, and so on. Reflect on whether you've experienced any of the following, even if only in fleeting moments.

THE NEARNESS OF AWAKENING

You've had times when your mind is calm and settled, with few or no thoughts.

You know what it is like to be without anxiety.

You've had moments of being very present and focused.

Memories, at least some, come and go without disturbing you.

You have felt open and curious about what comes next.

Your sense of self has expanded in an experience of beauty, awe, or wonder.

You have experienced a moment of spontaneous joy or bliss without warning or explanation.

You've had a sense of physical lightness.
You've had moments when your five senses seem heightened
and sharp.
You know what it is like to feel free.

Only a few of these experiences can be called exalted, but, when
they are, awakening is giving you a very strong hint about how close
it is to you. It would be impossible for awakening to be outside everyday experience; after all, being aware is universal. No one can live
in total unconsciousness.

A PATH FOR ALL

Living from a place of simplicity has a great advantage. This is especially true on the spiritual path. The path can become too complicated to follow when it involves the arcane teachings of an ancient
tradition like Zen Buddhism, Yoga, or Kashmiri Shaivism. In its essence, however, awakening *is* simple. It only involves paying attention, which everyone knows how to do. With no other requirements,
this is potentially a path for all.

The tricky part is that the attention we pay to things in everyday
life doesn't lay out a path. They are too jumbled and tangled up with
routines, habits, and memories. If we look to the end of the path,
awakening is about being aware of awareness, but that's not much
help. Unlike a musician who can practice scales on the way to becoming a virtuoso, awakening is a quantum leap. It transcends whatever you are thinking and doing right now.

Suddenly, a simple path has become baffling. A task like getting
breakfast on the table or driving your car to work requires your attention. Where's the room for paying attention on the spiritual path?
The answer has been called "second attention," which is present all
the time, no matter what you are thinking or doing. (Second attention calls on simple awareness—they amount to the same thing.)

Trying to pay second attention doesn't work. If you try to be aware
of awareness while frying an egg or negotiating traffic, your mind

will be divided. It is unlikely you'll be good at either attention. Many have run into a dead end because of this problem of the divided mind. Despite our best intentions, the spiritual path is self-defeating if we set it up as a special project. Our minds are already fragmented, torn between splintered forces in a world of opposites: good and evil, right and wrong, selfish and altruistic, desirable and undesirable. Tossing the spiritual path into the mix simply adds another opposite: spiritual and worldly.

To get past this obstacle, you have to realize the reality of what Buddhism calls "non-doing." Non-doing isn't passivity. It is a state of openness that allows your deeper awareness to do all the work on the spiritual path. Nothing can awaken you except awareness itself. Think of this like the healing response in your body. When a cut, bruise, headache, or sprained tendon heals, you don't participate in the healing process. The healing response acts independently. The same is true of awareness. It awakens you independently of whatever you happen to be doing.

This fundamental concept turns out to apply everywhere. Seen clearly, your mind is operating on its own. So are your brain and central nervous system, your respiration, your heartbeat, and the private life of every cell. You can intervene through conscious action, naturally, but lacking an intervention, non-doing rules your life at this very moment.

The following pages will explore how awareness takes over the awakening process and the various milestones along the way. Every awakening is intimate and personal, but there are aspects all awakened people share (such as the list of experiences on page 6). Yet this sounds suspiciously like passivity if you are just standing by, the way we stand by while getting over a cold—there's nothing you can do to speed up or retard the healing process.

How do you even know if awakening is happening? There is a way. When you contract an illness that requires medical attention, a doctor steps in to aid the body's healing process. The most effective interventions align with nature, and it is perilous not to align with nature. Current cancer treatments that use radiation and chemotherapy are painful examples of being forced not to align with the healing response. In fact, they compromise it and sometimes brutally assault it.

When you look at this issue from the Vedic tradition in India, there is spiritual alignment and non-alignment. Spiritual alignment brings a flow of true knowledge, or *vidya,* to a person. Non-alignment blocks this flow and condemns a person to remain in ignorance, *avidya,* of their true nature. Non-doing isn't passive, because you align yourself with the awakening process. By opening a channel to higher consciousness, you let awakening happen. It's a classic example of not trying to steer a river; the river will get you to your destination on its own.

EXTENDED WELL-BEING:
THE CHOPRA WELL-BEING INDEX

If non-doing is starting to become clear, there remains a mystery that cannot be solved. It's the mystery of what happens next. You are motivated to wake up. You accept that the path involves paying attention and simple awareness. What then? No one can predict what happens next. The path isn't a straight line; its course is unique to each person. To really grasp how the path is unfolding, you'd need to ask about a person's entire life, body, mind, relationships, purpose, and spirituality.

A decade ago, I set out to construct a meaningful survey to assess all these aspects. The result, the Chopra Well-Being Index (CWI), can be found in the appendix. You can assess your overall well-being by answering the questions that comprise the Index. The results will interest you, but there's a larger purpose. When you allow awareness to do all the work of awakening, it doesn't confine itself. Everything about you is governed by awareness at the deepest level. Awakening is like the Oscar-winning movie titled *Everything Everywhere All at Once* in real life.

Your individual consciousness, like a wave in the ocean, is connected to the infinite field of consciousness. You are cosmic in your true nature. Therefore, awakening leads to a very expanded version of well-being. The CWI gives you a picture of well-being that improves and expands as awakening gestates. Regularly returning to answer its questions again will give you a map of your progress.

I wanted the CWI to be statistically valid, and it was put through rigorous independent analysis and research. One outcome refers to spiritual well-being in particular. The vastness of spiritual experience is impossible to comprehend. Every age and culture hold a treasury of stories about awakening, which is the foundation of the lives of saints, seers, sages, and avatars.

But, statistically speaking, there are only a handful of questions that determine where you find yourself spiritually.

- Have you reflected on how your actions affect the world?
- Have you felt like you are part of something bigger than yourself that includes everyone else?
- Have you felt like you are more than just your body and mind?
- Have you felt connected to something larger than yourself, however you understand it?

Everyone falls somewhere on the spectrum of responses to these four questions, from outright denial or indifference to unqualified endorsement and acceptance. Of course, details matter. Every imaginable kind of spiritual experience has been reported. Here we get only the common denominator. When validating this part of the CWI, there was considerable overlap with social and mental well-being. That helps to confirm that awareness is all-encompassing (i.e., everything everywhere at once).

People who feel connected to a higher power also feel connected to humanity and the world as a whole. They feel a sense of presence that might be called divine, yet which comes from a child or the face of a wise elder. Their minds aren't confused by a disorganized storm of thoughts and feelings. Even when most active, their minds sense a backdrop of silence that is unchanging.

———

IN THIS OVERVIEW, YOU'VE met the themes that will evolve and expand in the rest of the book. Words can't convey, however, the fascination of knowing who you really are. Mystery meets revelation. The present moment confronts timelessness. It wasn't poetic license to call the promise of awakening eternal. As an epiphany, nothing can surpass the realization that your true nature is infinite and unbounded. At that point, a second life, the awakened life, can be lived in full.

2.

Your
True Nature

•

AWAKENING IS RADICAL. IT REVEALS A HIDDEN REALITY THAT cannot be penetrated by the five senses. The mind cannot think its way to get there. A classic analogy compares waking up to sitting in a dark cave and turning around to be suddenly blinded by a bright light. But what is most radical about awakening isn't that it is blinding, and it's not necessarily sudden. The process is natural, and it unfolds in perfect timing to what each person needs.

Flashes of awakening have come to be known as "peak experiences," moments of revelation that alter a person's outlook—on the world, everyone in it, and the nature of reality—all at once. Peak experiences fade but leave an indelible impression. Such experiences always reveal the light, never the darkness. Something about eternal love, the presence of the divine, confidence in a cosmic plan, or an awesome sense of the infinite is conveyed.

Full awakening makes these realizations feel like foregone conclusions. The surprise of a peak experience isn't present, but the outcome is. What is harder to put into words, because it is so intimate, is that awakening reveals everything in terms of you. Knowing your true nature, you know the essence of reality. The closest that words can come is this: Your essence is infinite unbounded consciousness, which we can call "pure consciousness." *Pure* means that consciousness remains quiet and unmoved within itself, not yet filled with any content of the mind.

To go back to a more familiar concept, pure consciousness is simple awareness taken to infinity. Hidden from the five senses, pure consciousness immerses you in an invisible field that is the source of everything in creation. Every page that follows will expand on this cosmic statement. In this case, the cosmic is also personal. Your source is the same invisible field of pure consciousness as the stars and the galaxies. You, like everyone else on Earth, spring from a source you cannot see or touch, yet without pure consciousness, human awareness would be impossible.

At your fingertips you now have the answer to an age-old question, "Who am I?" You are an expression of pure consciousness. When this truth fully sinks in, your life will be transformed. You will find a secure, unshakable place to stand in the field of pure consciousness. You will still be an individual, like a single wave moving along the surface of the ocean, but you will identify with the whole ocean. "I" and "All" become interconnected in a way that redefines your sense of self. Once you make this connection, you can never be the same person again.

This concept doesn't strike everyone the same way. It might feel breathtaking, confusing, or both. To a skeptic, it will be preposterous. To a religious fundamentalist, it will be heresy. But the chain of human evolution has inexorably led us here. Awareness is hidden behind the mask of matter. A cell looks like a microscopic balloon filled with salt water and specks of organic chemicals. If you shake the balloon, the chemicals should swirl around randomly, and if two random molecules are interactive, they will bond the instant they meet. But that is never the outcome, no matter how actively you move your body. A single cell cannot survive without performing thousands of precise chemical reactions per second.

Cells know what they are doing, which can only happen through being aware. The most primitive algae and bacteria regulate their inner chemistry. They react to their surroundings, responding to heat, light, food sources, and the like. To do that requires awareness of their surroundings. Only a few minutes into the subject, and already some qualities of pure consciousness are being expressed: awareness, organization, self-regulation, and orderliness. Whenever any quality of consciousness appears, the trail leads back to the source—this is true of all life on Earth.

Higher life-forms express more evolved awareness. Watch a house cat hunt, bond with another cat, seek dominance, and perform its mating ritual. We label all of this as instinct, but an instinct is just awareness that has been fixed in the genes. In your genes is the instinct for walking upright, using your opposable thumb, talking, and reading. Those genetic imprints can't be separated from awareness. Saying your first word is inconceivable without inherited awareness.

No matter where you look, the connection with consciousness holds fast. An elephant can look in a mirror and see that the reflection in the mirror is itself. That's a huge step in awareness from a parakeet, which looks in a mirror and is fooled into thinking that its reflection is another parakeet.

Keep in mind that we are talking about the evolution of consciousness, not Darwinian or physical evolution. In the wild, when an elephant dies, the rest of the herd gathers around the body, touches it with their trunks, and may remain with it for extended periods. Elephants have been observed gently nudging or standing vigil near the deceased, and they sometimes cover the body with leaves or branches. These actions indicate an awareness of death and a strong emotional bond within the herd. Whether we should say that elephants mourn their dead is an open question, but it is secondary to observing that they are aware.

Our common ancestor, *Homo erectus,* harnessed fire sometime between 400,000 and 1.5 million years ago. It is hard to imagine such a feat without possessing a mind, since all other creatures would instinctively run away from fire, not gaze at it and decide that fire was useful. Two qualities of pure consciousness were making themselves glaringly evident: intelligence and creativity.

The evolutionary step that made *Homo sapiens* fully human was self-awareness. Of all life-forms on Earth, we alone know that we are conscious. No specific date for this game-changing breakthrough can be determined. But, in an evolutionary burst of lightning, sophisticated cave paintings appeared around the world, and it is impossible to imagine a painting without being able to name the bison, deer, or bear being depicted. Even more astonishing is this: With our higher brain already in place when hunter-gatherers had only spears and flint blades, the capacity to build a cathedral, organize a religion, and calculate E = mc² was also in place.

So was awakening, which is reported in the most ancient Vedic scriptures of India. In Sanskrit *Atman* refers to pure awareness as it transforms from being infinite to being human. The first reference to Atman is in the Rig Veda, which is speculatively dated to around 1200 to 1500 BCE. That would date its first usage around the time that ancient rabbis were compiling the Hebrew Bible, or Old Testament. *Atman* originally meant "self," but evolved to mean self-awareness that goes beyond the individual mind.

What this means is crucial to awakening today. As early as anyone was writing about what it was like to be human, it was possible to say, "I am Atman," which is the same as "I am pure consciousness." I realize that things have turned very abstract very quickly. "I am pure consciousness" is such an overwhelming truth that we resist wrapping our minds around it. Even the vocabulary of consciousness is foreign to most people—philosophers deal in huge abstractions while the rest of us are immersed in the practicalities of daily life. The urge to avoid the subject entirely is not unusual. It is, in fact, a symptom of the very thing we are trying to heal: disconnection from our true selves.

At some point in our collective history, a light bulb went off, but there was no second light bulb to deliver the next bright idea about what awareness was meant for. Instead, a kind of supernova exploded in the human mind. A world of desires emerged, along with the means to achieve those desires, including peaceful means, like agriculture to provide food, and nefarious means, like rape, warfare, and violence. It has taken roughly 30,000 years for every aspect of civilization to evolve into the modern world, which is a miraculously short period of time.

In that period, we gained the dark and the light side of self-awareness. We became the first and only creatures on Earth to say no to DNA as destiny. We, not our genes, are the ones who create our life stories, build our character, and have our thoughts. DNA is destiny for all other life-forms. A horse, a dog, an earthworm, or a blue whale cannot say no to its genes because their DNA encodes their essential nature. Our genes also encode our essential nature, which is awareness. Once you have awareness, you have choices, and once you have choices, you can say yes or no.

Strangely, you can say no to the very consciousness that makes you human. Many do, and remain disconnected from their source. This is a tragic condition, like voluntarily walking back into prison. People display how disconnected they are by their unconscious behavior. In fact, we spend our lives amassing habits, beliefs, old conditioning, family traits, tribalism, political alliances, memories of old hurts, and more. The whole mass of unconsciousness limits your freedom, because once you become a predictable bundle of automatic reactions—always loving X but hating Y, making A your friend but B your enemy—you come closer to living on autopilot, a puppet of old experiences.

The result is the strangeness of our lives, which we accept as normal. It is normal to create weapons of mass destruction and Disneyland at the same time. We love operas that move us when the hero dies, and we don't blink an eye at the shocking murder rates in our cities or an accidental aerial bombing in the Middle East that obliterates a wedding party. We feel good about recycling but helpless to stop climate change.

All of this reveals the paradox of human existence: the profound potential of pure consciousness contrasted with the unconscious patterns that dominate our lives. The truth that pure consciousness is your essence and source is not actually an abstract truth. It is a call to remember who you truly are by reconnecting with the source. Without reconnecting, the conflict and confusion of our lives persists. Restore the connection, and you unlock the potential to live fully, consciously, and authentically.

3.

Maya, or the Waking Dream

•

TO THE AWAKENED, EVERYONE ELSE IS UNDER THE SPELL OF A dream. Unlike dreams at night, the all-embracing dream that we are immersed in is a waking dream. You can't tell that you are trapped inside it. The normal activities of life—thinking, speaking, and doing—proceed whether you are spiritually awake or asleep, which sounds confusing, but there is a huge difference. In the waking dream, everyone is partially conscious and partially unconscious. Although we accept this as normal, the hidden reality of our true nature comes through like a fuzzy, intermittent radio signal.

We were designed to be in contact with our true nature. Higher consciousness, therefore, is a birthright. It potentially belongs to everyone. Throughout history a few voices have spoken up to expose the waking dream.

"This place is a dream. Only a sleeper considers it real." (Rumi)

"The world, like a dream full of attachments and aversions, seems real until the awakening." (Adi Shankara)

"Regard this fleeting world as a star at dawn, a bubble in a stream, a flash of lightning in a summer cloud, a flickering lamp—a phantom, and a dream." (Buddha)

Against these isolated voices, even when they are revered, the physical world is too overwhelmingly real to be accepted as a dream. If awakening didn't exist, no one would ever know.

Telling people that they are walking around in a dream isn't likely to sound convincing—after all, the moment we get out of bed, we believe we are awake. Still less convincing is it to suggest that everyone is being fooled by an illusion or that they have fallen under a spell. All these terms are wrapped up in the concept of *Maya*, the Sanskrit word whose basic meaning refers to the power of manifestation or appearance. The appearance of everything in creation is Maya.

The great magician Harry Blackstone famously made an elephant disappear onstage, and it would shake our faith in the physical world if that happened in real life. But the world of appearances is already shaky in its dependence on illusions. For thousands of years, life proceeded without regard for atoms and molecules, gravity and electricity. The fundamental forces and building blocks of nature constitute a level of reality hidden from the five senses. Although physical objects, including this book, appear solid, at a microscopic level they are mostly empty space. We don't pass judgment on atoms and molecules because they are invisible, and there's no need to pass judgment on Maya. Maya exists for the same reason as atoms and molecules—to help us understand that perception is unreliable. Every schoolchild knows this from stories about the Earth not being flat and the sun not rising and setting in the sky.

But Maya runs much deeper. It poses a radical challenge to perception by saying that we don't experience what our bodies are, what the objects around us are, and what the entire universe is. In terms of Maya, what we perceive is merely the power of manifestation, the ability of pure consciousness to deliver a livable world aligned with the needs of human beings and other life-forms.

Perception is tricky because it shifts according to how you choose to see things; in other words, your perspective. When an airplane takes off on a flight from New York to Los Angeles, it is viewed differently depending on whether you are a passenger with a fear of flying, an excited child experiencing flight for the first time, a structural engineer of jet planes, an air traffic controller, a flight attendant, or the pilot. Their perceptions are tied to their perspectives.

Those perspectives are easy to shift by changing roles or jobs, but our perspective of the natural world is much tougher to change. To begin with, the five senses fight against us. They report physical sensations, not the creative activity of pure consciousness. The second obstacle is the mind, when it believes in the five senses, reinforcing a physical perspective. The thinking mind doesn't see its own bias, and eventually an entire worldview cements our unproven assumptions in place. That's why it is possible to say that Maya doesn't fool us—we are fooling ourselves.

Illusion, spell, and *waking dream* are interchangeable terms for the same thing: mistaking appearances for reality. Stage magicians fool the audience by using misdirection. A coin is palmed in the right hand by forcing the viewer to look at the left hand. Maya forces nothing, but our minds are misdirected away from the source, which is where creation happens. Since the source is you, the misdirection keeps you from being what you really are, a co-creator of everything in existence.

I prefer to think of Maya as an enormous distraction. The awakened life isn't about rejecting the world, but seeing through its distractions. We are constantly distracted by surface-level values—social status, material wealth, fears, desires—chasing happiness in possessions, achievements, or personal validation, unaware that these are just shifting appearances, not the source of lasting fulfillment.

Maya creates the physical world and takes it away. If that seems impossible, we must realize that the physical world is already winking in and out of existence, according to quantum physics. There's a mysterious portal at the quantum level. From this side of the portal, everything physical—including matter, energy, time, and space—vanishes from view. They cross the zero point of creation into what is known as a "virtual state." The virtual state is fascinating because it contains infinite potential, just like pure consciousness. The entire universe (and perhaps untold numbers of other universes) springs from nothing but invisible potential.

The crux of the mystery is this: Why prefer pure consciousness as the source of creation when physics already gives us the virtual state lying beyond the zero point? Because the quantum portal is mindless. So are the quantum field and every physical object. Nothing is aware—nothing can be aware—if you adopt a physical model. Only one special object, the human brain, is aware if you are a pure physicalist. But this is quite dubious. The chemicals that make up neurons can't think, and no one has ever shown to the slightest degree how atoms and molecules became aware in the 13.8 billion years since the Big Bang. The water in your coffee cup, the salt in the sea, and the sugar in sugarcane are mindless no matter where they are located, including inside your brain.

This gives us a clue, which 99.99 percent of neuroscientists ignore, that the brain might not know anything. The belief that your brain is thinking thoughts is just that, a belief. If you were told that TV sets create the programs they broadcast, that radios compose music, or that light bulbs invented light, you'd have no trouble seeing what an unfounded belief looks like.

But the assumption that the brain can think is workable, just as repairing a broken TV set brings back the picture. In reality, an orchestra plays music and uses a radio to deliver it. Consciousness has thoughts and uses the brain to deliver them. On a brain scan like an fMRI, the activity inside the brain perfectly matches the activity of thought, so neuroscience can proceed quite productively without challenging its unfounded assumption.

We don't need to challenge it here, either. However, we do want to know where thoughts come from, because that's an important part of the consciousness argument. As the much-respected writer on awakening, Rupert Spira, puts it, "Only awareness is aware."

A simple thought experiment gets us where we want to go. Imagine the moment a sperm fertilizes an ovum, creating the full complement of DNA for a future newborn. DNA contains only five chemical elements: carbon, oxygen, nitrogen, hydrogen, and phosphorus. These elements cannot think, and they make up many organic chemicals that create things besides the human brain.

The fertilized egg starts to divide over and over, while at the same time turning into specialized cells. The first true brain cell appears between day 21 and day 28. No cell that preceded it can think, nor will it go on to think when it becomes a heart, lung, kidney, or skin cell. The first primitive neurons start to do remarkable things, turning into specific types of brain cells and traveling to the precise locations where those cells will congregate as motor neurons, parts of the cerebral cortex or the visual cortex, etc. However, at no time does a process occur that could be called awareness—except for one.

While those primitive brain cells were differentiating so precisely and traveling just where they were supposed to be, so was every other cell in the embryo. An extraordinary display of awareness, if that's what we want to call it, wasn't awarded as a special birthright to brain cells. Awareness permeates the entire body and continues after we are born.

So, the setup is exactly like an orchestra using a radio to deliver the music. Pure consciousness is using cells—all cells, not just neurons—to deliver awareness. There is no reason to believe that neurons are thinkers, any more than radios are musicians.

The only way to get past the brain's mindlessness, and the mindlessness of every atom and molecule in the universe, is to place consciousness at the source of creation. We return to Rupert Spira's earlier observation: "Only awareness is aware." This simple truth undermines all our belief in the material universe, going back to the Big Bang. Spira continues, ". . . any honest model of reality must start with awareness. To start anywhere else is to build a model on the shifting sands of belief."

What the medieval world called the Great Chain of Being— a hierarchy where all levels of existence are connected as expressions of a unified source, known as God—can be updated. Awakening reveals the unbroken link between you and your source. It isn't necessary to deny progress, science, and technology. They are the products of human consciousness, too. The only necessity is to stop fooling ourselves. Maya exists to make us investigate where creation comes from, and the trail inevitably leads back to pure consciousness.

·

33 SUTRAS

A TREASURY OF

WISDOM

"WHEN YOU UNDERSTAND pure consciousness, you understand reality." That kind of statement, which captures the essence of something and crystallizes it in a sentence, is known in India as a "sutra." Sutras are the foundation of an awakened life in terms of what is revealed directly from the source. For centuries they have been the main way that spiritual wisdom has been communicated. The sutra I just gave is an original; it doesn't quote any ancient text.

But it serves the same purpose, which is to wake up your awareness. In Sanskrit the word *sutra* means "thread," and you can think of a sutra as a thread leading your attention back to your source. A sutra doesn't have to come from India's Vedic tradition. When Jesus said, "The Kingdom of Heaven is within," he uttered a sutra by condensing an important Christian teaching into a single expression. It was up to his listeners (and us as readers) to unpack all the meanings and implications in this sutra.

So, let's do that. "The Kingdom of Heaven is within" says, first of all, that Heaven isn't a place outside yourself. It's not God's perfect home above the clouds. By implication, if Heaven is within, so is God. Moreover, Heaven and God are inside everyone—Jesus's teaching has spread around the world, wherever Christianity has gone. Since we aren't normally aware that Heaven and God are within us, some kind of journey or process is involved to find this special place, and we need the teachings of Jesus to show the way.

That's quite a lot to unpack from six words. Sutras are very effective that way—they provide the essence of a truth in a few memorable words, and if those words really are true, a stream of meaning flows from them. In the best cases, the meaning that gets unpacked is profound and inspiring. This is what makes sutras precious in the Indian tradition. By contrast, an adage like "A stitch in time saves nine" from *Poor Richard's Almanack* is homespun and catchy, but there's not much to unpack. The adage means the same as "An ounce of prevention is worth a pound of cure." Helpful advice, but that's as far as it goes.

Sutras must also pass the test of truth. Everyday sayings, or adages, rarely do, or only get halfway. "Life is unfair," "You can't fight city hall," and "That government is best which governs least" don't pass the test of truth (even though Thomas Jefferson wrote the last saying). Instead, they express a strong opinion or belief. While such expressions may reflect common sense, like "A fool and his money are soon parted," sutras go beyond mere opinion. They are enduring guides that point us toward the infinite potential of who we truly are, serving as a foundation for profound understanding and transformation.

There is no doubt that truth is central to the Vedic spiritual tradition. Every Indian child knows the Sanskrit adage "*Satyam Eva Jayate*" (Truth alone triumphs), a saying found in an ancient Upanishad. From the Yoga Sutras comes a teaching, "When established in truthfulness, one ensures the fruit of actions." At the very heart of Buddhism lies the principle that all the phenomena reported by the five senses "are like a dream, an illusion, a bubble, or a shadow. The truth lies beyond these appearances."

This immediately raises the question, "What is truth?" For this book, there is no need to offer a textbook definition. We aren't going to rely on religious or spiritual traditions. Instead, this is going to be a personal journey into your awareness. The goal here is to wake up, because in waking up, you will see the truth. It will conform to the sutra that began this chapter: "When you understand pure consciousness, you understand reality." This isn't a question of belief. When an ancient teaching declares that our everyday life is "like a dream, an illusion, a bubble, or a shadow," it would take enormous powers of persuasion to get anyone—East or West—to entertain such a radical idea. My wife and children are real to me. It doesn't matter that Buddhist wisdom teaches that they are illusions.

Another sutra from the Christian tradition offers a clue about how to break through the natural resistance we feel when a radical idea threatens us. "And you will know the truth, and the truth will set you free." Set aside the religious implication that Jesus is the source of the truth. What I find powerful in this teaching is something else. Truth is assigned the task of setting you free. This holds a tremendous advantage for modern secular people. It isn't necessary to have faith, and the whole setup of organized religion is irrelevant for finding out, once and for all, what is real. (I hasten to add that religion has many beautiful and uplifting things to offer, just not in this context. There is the possibility in your journey, however, that you might discover that God is real.)

I've said enough to get us to square one, sparking the fusion of truth and reality. Don't feel obligated to accept anything so far. Only remain open to the possibility that you will know the truth when you see it. Nothing more is needed. As an Indian proverb goes, "A spark is enough to burn down a forest."

How to Read
the Sutras

THE SUTRAS THAT FOLLOW ARE ALL ORIGINAL, BASED ON MY experience in Vedic literature and my personal insights. I'm calling this section a treasury of wisdom rather than a story. No special order is marked out. These aren't steps in a journey—I've left the process of awakening to Part One and the assessment of your progress to the Chopra Well-Being Index as an appendix.

Sutras are meant to trigger your own insights. Therefore, feel free to sample these thirty-three sutras in any order you wish. A whole book could be written about each one, and in Eastern traditions whole books have been. But my aim is more modest: I want the reader to catch the experience of the awakened life as a kind of life-long epiphany. Wisdom is meant to be spontaneous and alive. A book can't accomplish this, because my words are fixed on the page.

But as one spiritual guide told me, you can smell the sea before you reach it. The smell of wisdom is delightful in itself, and, best of all, the sea stretches out just over the next horizon.

To be awake
Is to live close to your source

•

W HEN YOU FIRST ENCOUNTER THE PHRASE *PURE CONSCIOUSNESS,* it can seem beautiful on the one hand and baffling on the other. A cosmic truth might be revealing itself or yet another philosophical riddle to endlessly argue over. But reacting to the concept in any way, positive or negative, leads us in the wrong direction, because pure consciousness isn't a concept. It's not a mind-made idea but a fundamental reality in Nature. Just as the Earth's magnetic field causes a compass to point north, the field of pure consciousness draws the mind toward its source.

When you begin to align with your source, you start to wake up, meaning that your life becomes more conscious. We don't want to get lost in terminology here—what matters is experience. As you wake up, you remove the fog that masks your source like clouds hiding the sun. That's a classic image from the Vedic tradition of India. As the fog clears, something very real begins to happen. The qualities that you have been given from the source start to intensify.

If you walk around a big city, you will probably notice that your smartphone signal fluctuates—strong in some areas and weak or nonexistent in others. In much the same way, the most cherished qualities of pure consciousness, like love, seem to waver. When your mind searches for a "signal" of love, what happens? Some channels seem quite strong, such as a person's love of pets, which for many comes close to unconditional love. Other channels seem to be blocked—loving intimacy might be inaccessible perhaps because of past traumas or broken promises from other relationships.

In between these extremes, there's no clear channel. A young mother might feel a rush of unconditional love toward her newborn baby. She might vow inside to remain true to this feeling of unconditional love throughout her child's life. But as the child grows and becomes more independent, that mother's vow confronts other feelings—of anger, frustration, disappointment, heartache, or even alienation—that cause ruptures in loving parental relationships.

The source, however, only sends out unconditional love; the wavering of our feelings is due to poor reception, either because something blocks the signal, or we have moved too far away from the source. This can be verified through experience. Sit quietly with your eyes closed and bring to mind the most joyful experience of love in your life. Feel how blissful that moment was and also how you still long for it. What this simple exercise tells you is that love is generated inside you, not by an external person you love. The mere image of love in the mind brings the bliss that is attached to it. There can be no other location for love in all its forms except "in here."

Outwardly, life is complicated, especially when it involves relating to other people. But sitting alone, the channels to the source are more open and freer of obstacles. That's why we can *imagine* a perfect romance, great achievements, fame, the acclaim of others, a heart-pounding adventure. Imagination, a subtle form of creativity, is aligned closely with the source.

In the awakened life, your expectations rise because every desirable quality can be drawn from the source, like drawing water from a reservoir. You can draw a flow of creativity, because pure consciousness is infinitely creative. You can draw total security at the prospect of death, because pure consciousness is timeless. You can embrace uncertainty and a world of infinite possibilities, because pure consciousness is boundless, without borders.

Yet overriding any single quality, even love, is a sense of completeness. Pure consciousness is whole, and this holds out the promise of becoming a whole person. Modern life was foreshadowed more than

150 years ago by the farsighted Ralph Waldo Emerson when he wrote, "We live in succession, in division, in parts, in particles." Science was already subdividing the world into particles, which Emerson grasped even though he couldn't have foreseen billion-dollar accelerators blasting subatomic particles out of their hiding places for a few thousandths of a second.

Subdividing reality into smaller and smaller building blocks is the opposite of a truth that Emerson saw clearly, our essential wholeness. "Within [humans] is the soul of the whole," he wrote, "the wise silence; the universal beauty, to which every part and particle is equally related, the eternal ONE." That's the voice of someone who has joined a profound truth with his everyday reality, a perfect example of living close to the source.

Finding Your Wisdom

THE SOURCE AT YOUR FINGERTIPS

WRAPPING YOUR MIND AROUND PURE CONSCIOUSNESS is a challenge. You can't form a mental image of the infinite. In his book *New Seeds of Contemplation,* the Trappist monk and mystic Thomas Merton described the problem, using the word *God* instead of *source.* "If you understand Him, your understanding is not God. If you grasp Him, you have misunderstood. If you think you have captured Him, you are far from Him. For He is beyond all things and yet in them and in the midst of them, and yet beyond them."

Religions call upon faith and belief to get around the impossibility of grasping the reality of God. Consciousness, however, doesn't require either faith or belief, because we know for certain that we are conscious. The key is to draw so close to your source that its presence is immediate and accessible.

EXERCISE

Extend your forefinger over a surface such as a table or a page of this book. Move your fingertip close to the surface until very faintly you can feel its texture. Let your touch linger in order to feel the temperature of the surface. What has just happened seems so ordinary that you'd never pay attention to it.

In reality, however, you touched the infinite field of consciousness. How is that possible with merely a fingertip? In physics, as your finger touches the surface of a table or a book page, two energy fields interact: the energy field represented by your finger and the energy field of the surface you touched. In physics, it doesn't matter that you feel hardness, texture, or temperature. The two energy fields behave the same with two rocks or two particles of dust in space.

Fields are infinite and extend in all directions to the limits of the known universe. So, in one simple act, you touched infinity. There's only one thing missing. Fields in physics exclude experience. Words like *hardness, roughness, smoothness, coolness,* or *warmth* are meaningless when two fields interact. You have to add consciousness before any experience can exist. The field of pure consciousness is infinite, like the fields in physics.

Just like physics, when your finger touches a surface, a finite event is actually an encounter with infinity. It doesn't matter that we can't wrap our minds around the infinite. The infinite is making every experience possible from the moment we are born.

Everyday reality is a projection Of a world that is fragmented

•

DAILY LIFE GIVES US GLIMPSES OF WHAT IT FEELS LIKE TO BE awake. Such hints often come unexpectedly, during moments of perfect contentment when everything makes sense. You feel secure in yourself. The specters of worry about the future and bad memories from the past are dispelled. If you've had such an experience, perhaps in the arms of a beloved or gazing at a blissfully sleeping infant, your source is sending you a message: You are complete.

If you can sustain that feeling, you are experiencing wholeness. It's a simple, natural condition, one we are designed to embody. Wholeness isn't like the payoff of a diligent spiritual seeking or years of meditation. You are already whole. The difference is that now you realize it, a knowing that comes from direct experience.

What everyone experiences before awakening is fragmentation, the opposite of wholeness. Like slicing bread, the mind slices life into moments of fleeting perception, emotional ups and downs, successes and failures, satisfaction and disappointment. In fact, your mind believes that it has been assigned this duty to slice and dice. A life lived in bits and pieces of experience is the norm. This sad outcome was succinctly expressed by the noted spiritual writer Eckhart Tolle, who has observed that many people live burdened by a sense of separateness and isolation, caught in an illusion of division.

The word *illusion* is appropriate because only wholeness is real. The evidence is closer to you than breathing, in the intricate cooperation among trillions of cells in your body. No cell feels isolated, because the most microscopic chemical reaction is supported by the whole. It takes the mind to project a fragmented world. Because each fragment is isolated, the result is built-in conflict. Every desire is opposed by a counter-desire. You love to eat ice cream, but if you indulge too much, you feel guilty. You go to the gym to tone your body, which makes you feel proud, but skip a week, and the first sign of flabbiness makes you feel ashamed.

Immersed in the illusion, life becomes reactive, compulsive, ego-driven, self-absorbed, insecure, and anxious. You could recite more symptoms, but they all come down to a mind disconnected from the source. The isolated mind has no choice but to project its own fragmented state onto a fragmented world. The cycle is self-perpetuating.

Truth and reality come together in a quote from Thomas Merton: "We are not at peace in the world because we are not at peace in ourselves." Every spiritual tradition offers admonitions along the same lines, but there must be positive steps to take. This requires no recipe book but a straightforward principle: Any step that brings you closer to the source brings you closer to wholeness.

Each step occurs "in here" due to the nature of the mind. What is the mind? It is thoughts, emotions, imagination, and sensory experiences. For example, let's say I ask you to hear a sound in consciousness, like the sound of your mother's voice or John Lennon singing "Imagine." You hear those sounds even though there's no actual physical sound anywhere in your brain. The brain operates silently. What you hear are called "subtle sounds," which belong with the other subtle senses like subtle sight, which produces visual images in your mind's eye even though the brain operates in darkness.

These are fragmented experiences, but here's the important point: They are manifested from the same source, which is pure consciousness. As a backup to your computer, you can store thousands of images in the cloud, but pure consciousness doesn't have to do that. It doesn't store the sound of every mother's voice, or every visual image seen in the mind's eye for the whole history of *Homo sapiens*. Instead, all subtle experiences are part of the whole. The ocean doesn't need to count, name, and store every wave; the waves are part of the whole ocean. A single source generates infinite parts of itself simply by being conscious. It isn't conscious of X or Y or Z. It is conscious, period, before any content is created.

This isn't a mystical notion. Imagine the birth of a great painter like Pablo Picasso or a great composer like Johann Sebastian Bach. Baby Bach and baby Picasso aren't each a storehouse of the creations they will produce. They possess the *potential* to be great creators, and that's enough. Likewise, in the wholeness of pure consciousness lies the potential for every experience that every life-form, not just humans, will ever have—past, present, and future.

This realization sounds like a paradox. Pure consciousness is formless, yet from it, all forms are produced. But there is no paradox. The Big Bang was formless, a roiling chaos of energy so superheated it was too hot for matter to form, yet here you and I are, intricate expressions of form that evolved from the formless.

Your mind can get you out of that paradox, but it can't get you out of projecting a fragmented world. Your mind (or, rather, your brain) is caught up in the loop of projecting fragments, and the loop is self-perpetuating, like a hamster wheel. The wheel only stops turning when the hamster steps off it. It's not enough simply to think "I am not fragmented. This is just an illusion," because a thought about reality is not a force that can change reality.

There is another way. The hamster could stop running, a solution it doesn't hit upon because the animal is trapped in an involuntary reflex. You aren't—you have open to you many ways to slow down the mind until its activity is very subtle. Then you can rest inside the quiet and calm of the subtle mind. In time this settled state becomes your default mode, and the messages from pure consciousness start to come through more clearly. Those moments of feeling "I am enough; I am complete" start to expand, and through effortless evolution, you are so close to your source that it is like home. At that point, being awake is so natural that you don't question it or perhaps even notice the difference. All you can say for certain is that you are complete in yourself.

Finding Your Wisdom

REFLECTING ON THE TRUTH

TO KNOW THE TRUTH, ALL YOU HAVE TO DO IS SEE IT, NOT with your eyes but as a realization. There's a gap between what lies in plain sight and what we realize. In Hollywood romantic comedies, there's a turning point when the clueless hero finally looks at an obviously gorgeous, desirable woman and says, "I just realized something. You're beautiful, and I love you." There are also negative realizations ("How did I miss it? You only care about yourself"), but in every case, a gap is closed and reality hits home.

That's the same power of affirmations when they are effective. You suddenly see with an inner knowing what was right before your eyes all along. Below are three affirmations that pertain to wholeness and fragmentation. To use them, don't simply repeat each one mechanically, waiting until they sink in. Instead, be in touch with the part of yourself that *resists*. Then you are in touch with the gap of disbelief, skepticism, incredulity—anything that makes the affirmation seem wrong.

Here are the affirmations:

- I am not the fragments of the mind. I am the source that is whole, beyond all conflicts.
- I see the conflicts of the world without fear, knowing I am whole.
- I rest in the experience of being complete, free from divisions inside or out.

Don't challenge your resistance to these statements. Just be with it without judgment. Let it return to silence and wait. Keep your attention on one affirmation at a time. You are reflecting on the truth. If you do this with an open attitude, the deeper core of your awareness, which is closer to the source, will start to message you. Be patient. You can return to these affirmations as often as you like. You can stay with one as long as it takes. When realization comes, there's no predicting the form it will take. You might experience an "aha" moment or just quiet certainty.

This isn't a test; there is no passing or failing. The goal is simply to entertain a truth that brings you a sense that you are getting closer to the truth.

Any reality we can access Is a domain of consciousness

P ROJECTING THE IMAGES OF A THREE-DIMENSIONAL WORLD IS the mind's full-time job. The movie never ends. The brain gets to rest and renew itself during sleep, but even then images flicker through the mind in the form of dreams. There's nothing unique about this setup, until you ask an unspoken question: How can you prove that being awake isn't a dream, too?

Dreams are fuzzy, but so is the everyday world if you wear glasses and then take them off. Dreams flicker, but so does the everyday world if you are groggy and are about to fall asleep. Besides, there is the phenomenon of the lucid dream, a dream so vivid and lifelike that it passes the test for being real—until the dreamer wakes up.

It turns out that the really important point is also the most basic. Being awake, asleep, or dreaming in your sleep are all states of consciousness. Eight billion people walk the Earth seeing their own movies unfold, and no two movies are the same. But the movie projector is the same. To a movie theater, Hollywood sends new films every week, but they don't send new projectors with each one. Likewise, the light of consciousness works the same for everyone's personal reality.

The truth doesn't really sink in, however, until you realize that there is no movie that is separate from the projector. The analogy breaks down, because everything you see is consciousness on the move, endlessly creating new experiences. This truth upsets things in a major, even devastating, way. To be blunt, the modern world of science and technology depends on the opposite of the truth, namely, that consciousness is all in your head, and the world "out there" is the only objective reality.

For all practical purposes, everyone has adopted this assumption without question. It's part and parcel of living in a fragmented world. But the strict division between consciousness "in here" and the world "out there" is easily shaken. Here are a few ways to do that.

1.   See the color blue in your mind's eye. Now look out the window at the blue sky. Isn't the blue "in here" just as real as the blue "out there"? Yes, obviously.

2.   You are Isaac Newton sitting under a tree. An apple falls, and in a blinding instant, you understand how gravity works. What's the difference between how gravity works "out there" in the universe and how it works "in here" in Newton's mind? They are seamlessly connected, two sides of the same reality.

3.   The world's leading sex therapist has gathered hundreds of cases about romantic relationships. One day he sees a woman, and it is love at first sight. "My God," he exclaims, "I never thought it would feel like this!" No amount of objective data touches the reality of the real experience.

The examples could go on forever because experience is infinite, and every experience happens in consciousness. For the longest time, science refused to study consciousness seriously, taking it for granted, like the air we breathe. But a glaring fact began to loom in importance: No experiment can step outside the consciousness of the experimenter. This realization is enough to shatter the illusion of pure objectivity. All the more when it became part of quantum theory that the mere act of observing a subatomic particle isn't passive—it alters the reality of what the particle looks like, where it is located, how it behaves, and how it exists in time.

If you leave consciousness out of the equation, things like the "observer effect," as it is called, provoke one mystery after another. But if you accept that consciousness creates all experiences, there is no mystery. Our source is timeless, so it can manipulate time. Our source is formless, so it can manipulate space. Our source transcends the mind, so it can be viewed from any perspective you choose and be equally valid.

What applies to the source has to be modified for everyday life. Instead of being timeless, infinite, and formless, things are very different here on the ground. Time constantly passes, making every experience temporary and transient. The physical world is only accessible through the five senses, which are the tools of consciousness. They aren't reliable indicators of any permanent reality, just the provisional reality we've collectively agreed to accept.

That's why being awake is actually the same as having a lucid dream. In both cases, the setup is convincing. The mind is tireless at doing its full-time job of projecting a three-dimensional world. The same will be true of any reality we could ever perceive—it will be experienced in consciousness. Otherwise, it won't exist, not for humans, at least.

The main difference between a lucid dream at night and a waking dream is that you automatically wake up from the one but not the other. Being truly awake is a process we are undertaking in these pages.

Finding Your Wisdom

NOT "IN HERE," NOT "OUT THERE"

WHEN YOU LOOK OUT THE WINDOW AND SEE A TREE OR the house next door, it feels so real that calling the tree or the house part of a dream makes no sense. The whole point of the setup, as viewed from the source, is to make our waking dream livable. Practically speaking, it works well to locate the mind "in here"—the modern location is in the brain, whereas some ancient cultures placed the mind in the heart—and a tree or a house "out there."

If you were designing a convincing dream, you'd probably do the same, because it isn't practical for you to feel that you are bleeding into the scenery, losing the sense of a separate body in which a separate "me" resides. But this precaution has the undesirable effect of imprisoning us so that we will never know if a different reality, one where the unity of all experiences prevails, is possible.

This enforced limitation becomes a problem once you realize that in Eastern spiritual traditions the highest state of enlightenment is unity consciousness. It isn't a freakish or unlivable state but the natural outcome of being whole and escaping fragmentation. The upshot is that the division between "in here" and "out there" is arbitrary. You deserve to know, at the very least, that there is another option.

EXERCISE

To get a glimpse of another option, take a moment and imagine that you see a superhero flying through the air—it can be Superman, Wonder Woman, or any of the Marvel superheroes. From your vantage point on the ground, make the visualization as vivid as you can.

Now jump into the superhero's body and look down on the ground below. Feel the wind rushing through your cape, the vista of the landscape; feel the joy of flying.

Now switch back and forth. Put yourself on the ground as the observer, then up in the air as the superhero. Notice that you are effortlessly switching from watching a flying figure "out there" to an airborne perspective "in here."

The fact that you can do this shows that your consciousness is in neither place, neither "in here" nor "out there" but wherever you choose. You have experienced something essential about consciousness, that it has no fixed location. It permeates all locations. It allows for any perspective. No matter how you manipulate your point of view, consciousness itself doesn't change, just as waving a flashlight around in the dark doesn't change the fact that the source of its light is constant.

I am the expression Of my divine self

For almost everyone, pure consciousness isn't interesting until it becomes personal. Infinity is as impersonal as anything gets, and pure consciousness is infinite in all aspects—it has no boundaries but extends beyond space and time so that no matter how far you look, there is infinitely more to see. As an axiom from ancient India goes, everything you can conceive comes from a source that is inconceivable. You cannot wrap your mind around infinity because that's not how you experience consciousness in the first place.

You experience it as a stream of consciousness, one thought or sensation at a time. But this is an illusion, like saying that the way to watch a film is to break it down one frame at a time. If you go deeper, the stream of consciousness is like a mighty river. The surface, constantly moving and lapping at the shore, is endlessly active. Dive beneath the surface, and there are slower, stronger, steadier currents. Reach the very bottom, and the water is almost still—the molecules touching the riverbed might only vibrate faintly.

This simple analogy solves a profound problem: How can pure consciousness be unmoving and still while our personal consciousness is constantly on the move? Just as a river is made of the same water no matter whether the water is racing or still, consciousness is one thing, no matter how it moves and changes. This truth will become incredibly important as we move forward. For now, I'll expand on only one idea.

Your source is your divine self, and as it flows to the surface, you and everything in your life retains its divine quality.

You might be surprised that the word *divine* has appeared, but it is entirely appropriate. When pure consciousness is on the move, it carries its essential qualities with it. You love because pure consciousness is infinite love. You are creative because pure consciousness is infinitely creative. You are intelligent because pure consciousness is infinitely intelligent. I started by saying that infinity is impossible to grasp with the mind. But it is possible to move the other way, to gather together all the best in human existence—love, creativity, intelligence, compassion, mercy, justice, forgiveness, grace, and devotion—and attribute them to one God or the gods. In this way, the human becomes divine. If you start with pure consciousness, it's the same as the divine becoming human. Either way, it's the same.

Your divine essence is never lost, no matter what happens to you. What is never lost can always be regained. This applies to all 8 billion stories unfolding right now among people who are undergoing the extremes of pleasure and pain, good and evil, happiness and despair, wealth and poverty, along with every experience in between.

We saw before that the mind never stops projecting the dream we assume is real. The dream is convincing and livable, encompassing the five senses and the mind. But who or what flicked the switch that started the projector? Only pure consciousness has that ability. Think of the power plant that sends electricity to every household in a city to run all kinds of appliances. A light bulb looks nothing like a dishwasher, nothing like a stove. Once you know about electricity, those differences can be explained. Now go a step further. Imagine that a power plant sends current to every household, and the current *turns into* its appliances.

That's exactly what it means to project the three-dimensional world from the source. When you dream at night, everything is made of the same dream-stuff. It doesn't matter if the dream-stuff gives you a flying dream, a nightmare of toothy monsters, or a romance of love. Dream-stuff is turning into all those things. When you are awake, the reality you see all around you is more convincing, but it is also made of only one thing—consciousness-stuff.

That's a very hard sell in a society committed to the worldview of physicalism or materialism, where everything is made of one stuff, but the stuff has to be atoms, molecules, and subatomic particles. Yet reflect on this: If you have a dream of very, very tiny things like atoms or a very, very big thing like a galaxy, size doesn't change the fact that it is all dream-stuff and nothing but.

In our waking dream, everything is consciousness-stuff, which we can know personally by experiencing love, compassion, forgiveness, and every other divine quality. Remind yourself that this world is a projection, and it is the nature of consciousness to keep projecting. The dream never ends. So where do you go after death? A Buddhist dreamworld? A Christian dreamworld? An Islamic dreamworld? A Jewish dreamworld? They're all projections but with a more direct quality of the divine. You go where you want to, in the direction you feel guided to.

But when you are awake, you see the dream for what it is— a dream. This realization is important: Every world we experience, including projected heavens, *lokas* (Sanskrit for "planes of existence"), purgatories, realms of animals, realms of *pretas* or "hungry ghosts" (as the Buddhists call them), realms of celestial beings, realms of angels—all of these are projections of the infinite into the finite. Consciousness-stuff is their building material, and it sorts out the qualities of the divine self that each being identifies with.

Does it really help to be awake and know that every world, including imaginary ones, is a dream? It helps tremendously because you can identify with your divine self once the illusion of a separate ego-driven self has dissolved. The dissatisfaction of life is gone, along with the hunger for more and more. Rumi puts this beautifully: "The divine is not something outside of you. Look inside yourself; everything that you want, you already are."

Finding Your Wisdom

A DIVINE SPARK

THIS SUTRA UNFOLDED AS THREE DEEP TRUTHS THAT can be transformative. Sit quietly and let your mind absorb them.

- Everything I see is a projection of my divine self.
- I am the dreamer, the dream, and the awareness of both.
- In awakening, I find freedom from the illusions of separation.

As powerful as these expressions are, words can't substitute for experience. If the divine self is expressing itself as your life and everything in it, this means that the divine is always present. We don't have a constant experience of it because the waking dream is like a fluttering veil that shifts with every thought.

EXERCISE

You can experience a spark of the divine here and now. It is only necessary to find a calm, contented moment. You need to be free of distractions and alert, not sleepy before bedtime. Or tired from work. The next time you find such a moment, sit quietly with your eyes closed.

Place your attention on your heart. It should feel calm and settled. Now silently ask to feel pure joy, bliss, or ecstasy—the name doesn't matter. You can even do this without words. Just hold on to the faint feeling in your heart and have it expand into a feeling of joy. You might sense this as an expanding bubble or light.

It often helps to smile, encouraging the joy to rise inside you. For some, an image of a moment in the past that reminds you of joy is helpful. Getting the knack of it isn't hard, because, in reality, the state of joy is already there inside you, waiting to be noticed. You only have to gently summon it, and then you will have an experience reminding you of your divine self.

Embrace the unknown
And your burden will fall away

EXISTENCE IS MEANT TO BE LIGHT AND BURDEN-FREE. BEING here is the foundation of every moment of life, and being here isn't weighty, dark, anxious, or sorrowful. Consider the way young children approach life: They laugh without reservation, chase after bubbles as if nothing else mattered, and marvel at the texture of sand slipping through their fingers in a sandbox. In those moments, their entire existence is immersed in the now—light, free, and unencumbered.

We carry our adult burdens around because of a mistake. We mistake the known for reality when the known consists of vestiges of the past. Consider how the memory of a harsh word spoken years ago can linger, shaping how we see ourselves today. Or how a failure in the past makes us hesitate to try again, as if the past still defined the present.

We think we fear the unknown, the looming possibility of something terrible happening that we must protect against. But this is part of the same mistake, because everything we fear doesn't lie in the future. It is the repetition of past hurts, wounds, humiliations, losses, failures, and disappointments we already know and have stored away. Functional memory, like learning to cook or ride a bicycle, develops around a skill; it has no psychological burden attached to it. (Clinically, in rare cases where someone totally loses their memory and cannot even recall what happened a moment ago, functional memories tend to remain intact. The person still remembers how to get dressed, eat a meal, and go about daily activities.)

If the known isn't real, then only the unknown must be real. This realization turns everything on its head, because most people are afraid of the unknown. In the awakened life, however, you step into the unknown without anticipation or expectation—this may sound esoteric, but let's analyze what I mean by this. The known has already happened; it has vanished into memory or imagination and doesn't exist anymore. Yet the next instant in time must bring something, and what it brings is a new possibility.

A fresh thought or impulse, insight or desire, wells up in the mind. It comes from the field of infinite possibilities that is your source. The unknown is what allows for the emergence of everything new, fresh, original, and creative. A predictable life could be programmed into a robot, and human beings can't tolerate a robotic existence. Yet we go out of our way to make everyday life as predictable as possible. That contradicts the nature of life, which constantly renews itself. So why do we do it?

The most obvious answer is security. It feels secure to make your everyday life predictable. Once you set in place your fixed beliefs, opinions, habits, likes, and dislikes, much of your day can run on autopilot. You can shove your fear of the unknown out of sight. But to fear the unknown is to fear life itself. You can't have the good things that the unknown brings—all that is fresh, new, original, and creative—while also running your days on autopilot.

Then there is the effort it takes to carry around the burden of the past. Consider self-judgment. The harshest judgments we pass on ourselves often stem from guilt and shame rooted in past experiences. It is all too easy for external criticism to echo in our minds and turn into self-blame. Consider hyperthymesia, an extremely rare condition in which a person can recall every moment of the past with perfect clarity. One woman who suddenly acquired this remarkable ability was asked what it felt like. She answered ruefully, "I remember all the times my mother told me I was too fat." Her response reveals how vividly the past can haunt us, especially the painful moments.

Self-judgment is the dark side of the past in action, compelling you to live as though the past were still alive and real. Certain choices are cut off, those that painfully resemble whatever you are guilty or ashamed of, including body image, failures at school or work, unrequited love, bullying, social rejection, and so on. The waking dream that people are living is nothing if not convincing.

Countless possibilities are lost by repeating the known and fearing the unknown. And yet, at every moment, the source still gives rise to infinite possibilities. Every moment is a portal to freedom without burdens—this is literally the lightness of being.

Finding Your Wisdom

EMBRACING THE UNKNOWN

EVERYDAY LIFE IS CLOUDED BY FEAR OF THE UNKNOWN, and waking up from this part of the waking dream is a process. For some people a light bulb goes off—they see that the unknown has been needlessly labeled with anxiety when in reality it is actually the source of every new possibility. For most people, however, the whole issue is a bit like navigating barbed wire: It requires careful and deliberate steps.

The key is to stop avoiding the issue while remaining in your comfort zone. You have all kinds of options open to you.

Reframe the situation: Whenever something new and surprising pleases you, whether it is as simple as a restaurant dish you've never tried or as intimate as a loving gesture from someone you care deeply about, pause and say to yourself, "This came to me from the unknown." If a negative or jarring news story grabs your attention, say to yourself, "I'm caught up in something I've seen many times in the past. I care, but don't need to waste too much attention on it."

Become more creative: Creative pursuits are one of the best ways to explore the unknown. The greatest poems begin with a blank page, and the most beautiful paintings with an empty canvas. These starting points reflect life's essence—a need for renewal and growth that comes from an open and receptive mind. By embracing creativity, you transform the unknown into a source of inspiration.

Stop focusing on worst-case scenarios: Doomsday possibilities are phantoms from the past projected into the future. They give bad memories the power to frighten us through amnesia—we forget that we are the ones giving these memories power over us. When they arise, say to yourself, "That's not me anymore. I am here now."

Recognize the reality of now: Realize that the past and the future have no tangible reality compared with the present, where reality unfolds. Use memory where it is useful; don't let memory use you.

When you find yourself being distracted, stressed, or pressured, immediately give yourself a time-out. Find a quiet place, close your eyes, and breathe normally until you reach the state of simple awareness (see page 7).

Reframing uncertainty and staying centered in yourself are both important, so I hope you take seriously that fearing life's uncertainties isn't the right way to exist. Yet there is something more important when we limit our choices to safe, familiar ones. The motive is to make life manageable, yet the result is that we deny ourselves the expanded awareness that is the glory of the human mind at its most creative—open, receptive, curious, tolerant, and transcendent. Bit by bit, constricting your awareness robs you of your wholeness.

Wholeness is all-embracing, and once you attune yourself to that reality, your awareness expands. When you live with constricted awareness, on the other hand, you are watching life through a narrow window. There is only one way out: You must trust existence, meaning that you feel that reality is on your side, because whatever you want to do is good for you. Having reality on your side is the same as having deeper awareness on your side. At the source, you already know this. By expanding your awareness on the path of awakening, you exchange a narrow window for a panoramic view. Once you fully experience that reality is on your side, you will have accomplished the goal of every religion, metaphysical school, and spiritual tradition.

Because your source has infinite potential, So do you

•

As soon as you introduce the word *INFINITE* into a conversation, resistance rises, because it seems undeniable that everyone's life is limited, in other words, finite. This is part of the waking dream, which convinces you to choose limitation as if there were no other choice. It will come as a breakthrough to discover that your life has always been connected to the field of infinite possibilities that is your source. Your self-image should begin with the infinite, not with limitation.

Everyday life has vast potential we routinely take for granted. To start with the words we choose, an adult vocabulary contains on average between 20,000 and 30,000 words. How many sentences can be formed from this average number? The total is unimaginable. The best estimate, which limits a sentence to 10 words, is $20,000^{10}$ at the low end, which is 20 followed by 13 zeroes or 200 million million million million—that's not infinite, but it's a staggeringly huge number. Taking just the 5-word sentences, if you read a sentence every second, it would take you 10 million years to read them all. When you start talking about the possible connections your 86 billion brain cells can make, the number is more than double the stars in our home galaxy, the Milky Way.

The real point isn't these huge numbers, however, but your *poten-*

tial to choose words and formulate new thoughts. This potential exists at your source. In fact, your source is nothing but potential. It isn't a storehouse of every word, thought, or idea, like a cosmic dictionary or the cloud that stores digital information. You can take a child born deaf and mute who has no experience of language, and yet the potential is still there, and with the proper training, a Helen Keller can emerge with eloquent writing ability.

The closer you are to the source, the more intense this potential becomes, and not just for writing. There are three- and four-year-olds who can play the violin or piano at advanced levels, contradicting all known theories of how the brain develops in early childhood. When other children are just learning to tie their shoes, these prodigies are winning international violin competitions at six or seven. The only viable explanation for this is that the source has given them phenomenal potential. The same is true of child prodigies in math, who can be given a long number and told to find the cube root. They produce the answer faster than it can be written down by hand because they don't have to do any computation in their heads—the answer is given to them from the source. Srinivasa Ramanujan, a self-taught mathematical genius, credited a goddess named Namagiri with delivering him complex mathematical formulas in his dreams, formulas that later advanced modern mathematics.

In the field of infinite possibilities, human awareness is given access to infinite synchronicity, infinite unpredictability, infinite creativity, infinite correlation, infinite evolution. Potential is invisible. It doesn't register on the most sensitive scientific instruments because it exists in a domain all its own, beyond physical laws. Infinite potential exists in the fundamental, irreducible, causeless, unborn, spaceless, timeless, borderless, incomprehensible, and unimaginable domain that is pure consciousness.

From ancient India onward, terms like *boundless, spaceless* and *causeless* had to be devised for a special purpose. Nothing in Nature besides the source deserves these terms. The main reason that pure consciousness needs special words comes down to infinity, which most people think of as a big, big number. But it isn't. *Infinite* simply means "not finite"; in other words, having no limitations at all. If you count the biggest number a supercomputer can calculate at the highest speed, an infinite number will still remain to be counted. And so infinite potential isn't a big, big number, either. It is pure potential. It's your passport to the unknown, no strings attached. You have the choice to go everywhere or nowhere.

Some rare individuals take full advantage of their passport, particularly artists. Pablo Picasso created art in all forms—paintings, sculpture, collages, sketches, and pottery—at a furious rate, creating between 2.5 and 4 artworks per day throughout his ninety-one-year life. But it is more likely that someone will be frightened by too many choices; even a long restaurant menu creates hesitation and confusion for some people. The habit of treating limitation as normal has affected all of us. The pioneering psychologist William James wrote that our everyday, waking consciousness represents only a fraction of our potential mental life. He likens it to a "thin slice" of the broad spectrum of consciousness that is available to us.

The awakened life retrieves the infinite potential that is your birthright by giving you clear access to your source. Expanded awareness is its own reward, just as constricted awareness is its own punishment. Being closer to the source makes the fulfillment of any desire far more possible. But there is more to infinite possibilities that needs to be unfolded.

Infinity by its very nature must be complete; it cannot leave any possibilities out. Whatever you can imagine, plus a boundless number of things you can't imagine, exist in their own domains. This includes so-called supernatural worlds, all the heavens and hells, Tibetan Buddhist *bardos,* Vedic *lokas,* and on and on. In pure consciousness, there is no difference between the imaginary and the actual. Both emanate from the same source, even though we look upon the imaginary as more unreal. Alice goes to imaginary Wonderland; she meets fictitious creatures, not Queen Victoria using a flamingo as a croquet mallet. But such distinctions disappear when everything is swallowed up in the same waking dream. Are UFOs closer to Alice or to SpaceX?

The worlds that lie beyond waking, dreaming, and sleeping are accessed in specialized ways. Meditation with an intense focus on reaching other worlds can open up unknown portals. Visionaries have their own access, and some yogis are reputed to physically come and go to *lokas* due to yogic abilities known as *siddhis*. All of this sounds mystical and fantastic. You can approach the concept of unknown worlds with either skepticism or belief, but ultimately, what matters is the experience itself.

The potential for unknown things to happen—in *bardos*, here on Earth, or in Lewis Carroll's imagination—requires an invisible force of attraction. This force is *karma*, the Sanskrit word for "action." Karma turns potential into action. Almost everyone appreciates music, but our musical potential is parceled out very specifically into composers, professional musicians, amateur musicians, avid listeners, and so on. The difference between Mozart and a ten-year-old struggling with piano lessons is karmic.

Karma is not just a mystical force. It's the mechanism through which consciousness organizes and expresses itself in the material world. Unfortunately, the mind can't get much further with an explanation. With infinite potential on one side and the countless desires and inclinations of human beings on the other, every karma in a single person's makeup gets mixed up like all the grains of sand on all the beaches in the world. Theoretically, you could follow the interaction of every grain, but in practice, the chance is zero.

But karma is far from an empty concept. Because of karma, we aren't aimless wanderers in life. We have talents. We get interested in specific things and choose specific directions. Over the years we develop into individuals whose behavior fits into patterns. What karma represents is the ability of consciousness to shape itself into all of these patterns. A great deal of mystery remains, but if you want to explore other worlds, and you have strong enough karma in that direction, those worlds will actualize for you. As far as Yoga is concerned, that's how this world actualized for you the day you were born.

Finding Your Wisdom

THE KARMIC CONVEYOR BELT

IF YOU THINK OF ANY WORD—*OSTRICH, WIZARD, petunia*—you caused an invisible potential to emerge into the physical world. The same is true for the words you speak and the actions you take. Imagine this process being like a conveyor belt. A mental intention starts the conveyor belt running, the potential you want to materialize is instantly located, and it is carried to the surface to manifest physically.

If your desire reached all the way to your source, every intention would be fulfilled. Any potential would be actualized with a touch of the mind. (Yoga in all its forms, all of them directed at expanding awareness, exists to gain a greater ability to do just that.) But in everyday life, many desires don't come true. The conveyor belt runs into snags along the way; it runs into karma. Here, *karma* serves as a blanket term for influences from your past. Desires are frustrated by the interference of old traumas, outworn conditioning, self-doubt, half-hearted intentions, and inner conflicts.

Yet as frustrating and disappointing as life can be, karma doesn't have the upper hand. The limitations it imposes are narrow while the real you has infinite potential. It is important to know and affirm your essential self. The great Bengali poet Rabindranath Tagore expressed it beautifully in perhaps his most famous quote: "The same stream of life that runs through my veins night and day runs through the world and dances in rhythmic measures."

Sometimes the image of a conveyor belt is replaced by the concept of flow, as expressed by the Chinese philosopher Lao Tzu: "Let reality be reality. Let things flow naturally forward in whatever way they like." Reaching that state of equanimity requires a journey, and the first step is to accept your true nature as pure, infinite potential. You can do this in manageable steps every day.

In the face of challenges, don't focus on obstacles but look for clues that a solution wants to emerge.

If you find yourself resisting and pushing back in a situation, stop and pause for a while. See if the situation improves on its own.

Relinquish your desire to be in control.

Pay less attention to loud, insistent thoughts. Pay more attention to quiet thoughts that come in calm moments.

Learn the value of sitting in quiet reflection.

Don't make decisions when you are stressed, angry, or agitated.

See others as an expression of pure consciousness, just as you are.

Whenever good things happen, say to yourself, "I am close to the source."

To know effortlessly
Is the highest form of knowing

WHEN WE SAY THAT LIFE IS HARD, WE ARE SAYING SOMETHING unknown anywhere else in Nature. Animals inhabit the harshest environments on Earth—penguins in the Antarctic winter, mountain goats on sheer cliff faces, camels in the scorching Sahara—with perfect equanimity. They cannot imagine either a hard life or an easy life, only the life they naturally accept.

The hard lives that humans lead place us far from our source. Ultimately, the problem that brings so much struggle into common everyday existence is thought itself. Thinking is rife with conflict and confusion, doubt and delusion, wrong beliefs and stubborn blind spots. The solution is to find a way to tap directly into pure knowing.

Pure knowing is a built-in trait of consciousness. It doesn't require any intervention of thought. Everyone is familiar with thinking, so we don't need to spend much time on it. The thinking mind is with you from the moment you wake up every morning to the moment you fall asleep. But so is pure knowing, which I imagine will surprise you. Pause to consider how much of your everyday life is already turned over to consciousness by itself. In many areas consciousness functions perfectly well without thinking. Intuition, for example, is a form of intelligence that doesn't rely on deliberate thought, as are insight and higher spiritual experiences like revelation and epiphany.

Peak experiences and "aha" moments arrive spontaneously, without effort or planning, just as falling in love does. Similarly, imagination flows freely without needing to stay inside the boundaries of logic and reason; emotions rise and fall of their own accord without requiring conscious analysis. Meditation, which brings the mind closer to its source, is actively hindered by thinking.

Then there is the subject of character: Traits like kindness, loyalty, compassion, empathy, courage, and resolve don't arise because we consciously thought our way to them. Instead, they emerge naturally from who we are. The same is true of talents and gifts—they are expressions of our being, not the result of intellectual effort.

Going even further, pure knowing has taken care of you far better than thinking has. In the waking dream we call day-to-day life, we spend futile time and energy trying to have positive thoughts, suppressing our depressing and anxious thoughts, escaping memories of past hardships, and so on. The stream of consciousness, which adamantly resists being controlled, is like a beehive of thoughts buzzing constantly . . .

By discounting pure knowing, we disconnect from the silent, unseen potential of consciousness. We deprive ourselves of what consciousness can offer beyond the limitations of thought.

Now you can see how powerfully your life has been guided without the effort of thought, yet the issue goes much deeper. Rational thought makes claims that don't match the way the mind actually works. For example, most decisions are made emotionally, followed by rational explanations that pretend to be the cause. You know that you're sick of your old job before you think of reasons why it is bad and other reasons why a new job will be better. If you love someone romantically, you can list all the virtues that person has, but if you discover that you have been betrayed, a new list appears with all the positive traits replaced by negative ones. Any hot-button issue like religion, politics, or war can be filled with rational discussion to disguise that our orientation basically comes from the gut and often depends on primitive hatred or blind allegiance.

To expand rational thought beyond the areas where it is absolutely necessary—like science and technology—to areas where pure knowing actually does everything, is an illusion. The effort needed to think everything out all the time—worrying, foreseeing disaster, speculating about the future, regretting the past, fretting over relationships, turning countless molehills into mountains—is a primary symptom of duality and separation.

When the knower is separated from the known, the two worlds of "in here" and "out there" are created. Separation and duality are the same. They create a gap that we try to cross by constantly thinking. Take something as fundamental to human happiness as love. In pure knowing, the question "Does he/she love me?" is answered before it is asked. You simply know. In the condition of separation, the question is always up for speculation, gathering evidence, looking for telltale signs, and seeking reassurance—in other words, expending mental effort because you aren't connected.

DUALITY AND SELF-DOUBT

Duality gives rise to fundamental questions that make life confusing and make you personally insecure:

Am I worthy? This question suggests the possibility that you might not be worthy, creating self-doubt.

What do I lack? implies that you are incomplete or missing something essential.

Why don't things go my way? reflects a belief that life is unfair or working against you.

Who is on my side? hints at the fear of being alone or unsupported.

Am I safe? raises concerns about danger or vulnerability.

Do I have a future? reveals uncertainty or fear about what lies ahead.

What's wrong with me? suggests that there is something inherently flawed within you.

In all these cases we mistake thinking to be the solution when, in reality, it is the cause of the questions. Only by ending duality and separation does the mind know how naturally it is designed to operate, through pure knowing.

Pure knowing increases in the awakened life, and the awakened life is achieved by getting closer to the source. The essence of pure knowing, as it exists in pure consciousness, is *gyana* in Sanskrit (sometimes written as *jnana*). Gyana is what allows you to know anything in the first place. It increases when you trust your intuition, when you meditate, when you make conscious choices, and when you reflect on wisdom in the form of these sutras.

Gyana isn't infected with the bad habits that effortful thinking has instilled in us. It looks at situations holistically, not one piece at a time. It doesn't have a win-lose orientation. It goes beyond linear cause and effect. The full light of gyana at the source is like eavesdropping on the divine mind. When you have pure knowing, you know pure joy, because joy is wrapped into it as bliss-consciousness, or *Ananda* in Sanskrit. One could keep on itemizing its benefits, but, simply put, all are the outcome of experiencing your whole mind instead of a fragmented mind.

Pure knowing happens before a thought arises. It resides in the field of all possibilities. You know what you need to know in the moment without anticipation, without regret, and without the use of memory. By comparison, the thinking mind wanders in its self-created wilderness.

Finding Your Wisdom

INTUITION IN THE MOMENT

INTUITION IS MUCH MORE OF A BLANKET STATE THAN WE realize. The common image of intuition is like a bolt out of the blue, a sudden realization usually reserved for people who consider themselves especially intuitive. In reality, intuition is a steady state, and when you are in that state, you experience direct, effortless knowing. Consider driving a car: Experienced drivers don't think about the mechanics of driving—they just do it. In a crisis some people will take to the open highway for an aimless hour or two where they enter an almost meditative state, free of outside concerns. Because intuition is a kind of pure knowing, it doesn't come in the form of words in your head; in fact, if you have a thought, it can't be an intuition. At best, it can express a feeling that came before, and feeling is often intuitive.

It would make life simpler if formulas like "trust your gut" or "go with your first thought" worked, but, for most people, intuition is blocked, and getting past the blockage creates confusion. For example, fear isn't intuitive. Intuition tends to feel calm, clear, and expansive, while fear feels urgent, heavy, and contractive. Yet a fear reaction is quite common in the face of a difficult choice or time pressure. Intuition never applies pressure, because pressure is stress.

The recipe that works best is to become familiar with the intuitive state. This isn't difficult per se, because the only requirement is an open, calm, and relaxed mind. When your mind is in this state, you aren't distracted by having an expectation or anticipation. You are prepared to receive a subtle impulse from close to the source. You will know such an impulse because it feels light, natural, effortless, and satisfying.

None of these elements are alien to you; you just need to put them together. Here are a few exercises that encourage and enhance the intuitive state.

- At the end of the day while you are still alert and not sleepy, sit quietly and reflect on the very nicest moment of the day. Don't think back. Just sit and allow the moment to come to you. There is no right or wrong. You just want to experience the mind responding without the effort of thought.

- Sit quietly and reflect on the nature of love. Simply have the intention, then let your mind bring you anything that comes up. This exercise allows you to experience flow.

- Sit with pen and paper. At the top of the page write a simple trigger phrase, such as "I am," "I feel," or "I am going to." Then write for 5 to 10 minutes without lifting your pencil from the paper. Don't rush or force. Just let the words come to you automatically. When you finish, ask yourself how the experience felt, and look over your writing to see if something meaningful jumps out. This exercise is about trusting that your intuition has a message for you.

- A variation of the above exercise is to write one of the following questions at the top of a page: "What do I need to know?," "What do you have to tell me?," or "Am I missing something here?" Then proceed as above and write for 5 to 10 minutes without lifting your pencil. This is a more advanced use of intuition because you are asking for knowledge you didn't consciously have before you began. Look over your writing at the end and feel how much or how little you trust what came through. This is a good exercise to repeat a few times over the course of a week. It takes repetition to open the channels of communication with your pure knowing.

SUTRA 8

Your everyday self Is your essence in disguise

EVERYONE HAS A GREAT GIFT BESTOWED BY PURE CONSCIOUS-
ness, an individual self. At the same time, that gift is misunderstood
and misused. This occurs when we regard the self, or "I," as a thing,
a separate, isolated entity. We can point to Maya as the root of
this mistake, but a big part is played by ordinary life. We talk about
going it alone and looking out for number one. People seek self-
improvement like getting a better model of car, and relationships can
come down to a kind of consumer shopping until you find "the one"
who is the best fit with you.

Reality couldn't be more different. Maya exists, as we saw, to expose how pure consciousness manifests itself in creation. This process
applies to you. Our essence is pure consciousness, which undergoes a
process in order to create your individual self. By design there isn't a
gap between the two. The line of communication is kept open for the
simple reason that your self keeps evolving. You aren't finished and
placed in a workshop window like a puppet. You are part of the process of creation every moment of your life.

It isn't hard for people to see this as the big picture. With a moment's reflection, we know that "I" is no longer a helpless infant, a
toddler, a first grader learning to read, and so on. The process of
evolving is obvious, and the self is right in the thick of it. Yet after
seeing the big picture, people still cling to many aspects of thing-ness
about themselves. There is the phrase "My body, myself," which iden-

tifies with physical appearances. Personality isn't visible like the body, but decades can go by and a pessimist is still a pessimist, an introvert still an introvert, an anxious personality still anxious.

I'm not trying to encourage value judgments about how others choose to live, only to point out that when you identify with any sort of thing-ness, you are losing connection with your essence. You stop, or at least inhibit, the evolution of your consciousness. The waking dream is co-opting your very sense of self. Society reinforces our attachment to thing-ness with labels like rich or poor, Protestant or Catholic, high school graduate or college graduate. The self gets buried beneath these tags, like a kiosk plastered with public notices. One person is labeled as rich, privileged, a doctor living in a big suburban house, while another is marked as poor, a cleaner renting in the inner city as a single mother with three children. These labels obscure the deeper truth of who we are.

If you take away all the differences in every stage of life, every experience has a common quality: "I am." "I am" is not the person. "I am" is the awareness in which the person, and the scenery that goes with the person, arises. "I am" is your ticket to participate in infinite awareness. Therefore, awakening involves waking up from the identity of being a separate, isolated person.

Your sense of self needs to be stripped down and simplified. Maya disguises your essence in layers of personality, ego, everyday duties and desires, memory, and the social tags touched on already. Yet it is understandable that "I am" feels at first blush like a poor substitute, an abstract concept with very little savor. Actually, the opposite is true. "I am" gives life the flavor of experience. In moments of pure joy, ecstasy, revelation, and rapture, everything about your disguise falls away, and the light of pure awareness shines through you. That's what it feels like when nothing obstructs your essence.

Let's see if we can get thing-ness out of the way once and for all. Imagine that you are a pebble in the middle of the stream of life. Experiences flow past you, which you feel without trying to hold on to them or possess them. Now imagine that the pebble shrinks until it is a speck, and then the speck becomes invisible. Nothing else has changed. Life constantly flows around you. Now that you aren't even a speck, you have the freedom to experience anything without holding on to it or possessing it. In other words, you aren't weighed down by the past. Freedom is your permanent state in the here and now.

THE REAL POINT IS THIS: The invisible speck is indistinguishable from the flow of life. The flow isn't happening around it. It isn't happening to it. In, out, and around are merged without a boundary to separate them. When you can say, "I am the flow of awareness," you are speaking as your essence. External changes can take place, like the external changes the physical body undergoes, but you will regard them as part of the passing scenery. Your everyday self will be part of the passing scenery, too. I'll hasten to add that none of this comes from the pages of mysticism: Real people, here and now, report the kind of transformation we've been talking about.

It is their firsthand experience. They also report what is often called the lightness of being. The awakened no longer carry the burdens that weigh down the self-as-personality. Because this change occurs "in here," people who lead an awakened life continue to play their roles at work, in relationships, and in the family. If external life changes, the force that creates those changes is karma, which grinds out the interactions of cause and effect. The main thing isn't karma, however. It is freedom. It is waking up.

Finding Your Wisdom

"I AM"

W E DON'T USUALLY SAY THE PHRASE "I AM" BY ITSELF but rather follow it with something else: "I am X." X can be anything. I am happy, I am late, I am graduating next month. By itself "I am" acquires a special meaning when there is no X—you simply state that you exist. Since you can't say anything without being aware, the full meaning of "I am" is "I exist as a conscious being." That's not only your essence but the key to waking up from the disguise imposed by Maya.

You can peel away the disguise one layer at a time with a simple thought exercise. Sit quietly and think of your name and a brief description of yourself. Then repeat, taking away words until you are left with only "I am." In my case, it would go like this. *I am Deepak Chopra, an Indian doctor in America. I am Deepak Chopra. I am Deepak. I am.* When you arrive at the end, sit and absorb the impression of the open, quiet mind that the words "I am" make.

The impression is fleeting, but it gives you the experience of not needing to think about anything beyond a steady state of awareness. You might imagine yourself sitting alone in a room. You feel calm and centered, at peace. The room expands to an auditorium. You still feel calm and at peace. The walls of the auditorium melt away, and you are sitting in the middle of the night sky surrounded by stars. These too fade away, and now you are at the center of creation. There are no objects around you. There doesn't need to be. It is enough that you are aware of being at the center of creation.

Finally, to gain a sense of flow as consciousness manifests itself without end, sit and deliberately try not to meditate. Let your mind be as active as it wants to be with thoughts, sensations, memories, and anything else that comes to mind. Ordinarily, this stream of consciousness carries meaning with it. The words and memories mean something to you; they have relevance.

Perceive it differently this time. Look upon your mental activity as so much buzzing in your head, paying no attention to any meaning at all. This takes a little practice, but when you get the knack, you will be witnessing your mind from the viewpoint of "I am." The activity of the mind is just part of the scenery, but you are not. You are the still point of pure awareness that needs nothing but itself to experience fulfillment.

Consciousness has no origin story, So neither do you

·

B IRTH IS A WORD THAT CONJURES UP OPTIMISTIC FEELINGS while *death* arouses fears, but in any case, we can't do without them. It's an unbreakable rule in Nature that things start and end. But pure consciousness is exempt from the rule. Being at the source of creation, consciousness has no source itself. You can't make up an origin story for something that "is now and ever shall be, world without end," to quote an important hymn from many Christian liturgies. The words apply to God, who is the religious expression of an eternal, infinite source that has no source itself.

Few people walk around pondering these kinds of metaphysical questions. For most of us, eternity won't be an issue until after we die, and perhaps not even then.

Everything changes, however, if birth and death are just another part of the waking dream. To all appearances, the physical body is born, matures, ages, and dies. Nature's rule that everything must have a beginning and an end seemingly applies until you ask, "Who am I?" at which point consciousness is inescapable. You cannot say "I am" without acknowledging "and I am aware."

There is no evidence that awareness began at any point in time. This holds true for the entire known universe as well as for a nine-month pregnancy. To the newborn cosmos or a newborn baby, birth is physical—the evidence for that is indisputable—but no one can prove the birth of consciousness. Millennia ago, in an age of faith, the lack of proof posed few problems for believers. As the Bhagavad Gita declares, "The spirit is neither born, nor does it ever die; nor having once existed, does it ever cease to be. The spirit is without birth, eternal, immortal, and ageless. It is not destroyed when the body is destroyed."

These were comforting words across the eras when infant mortality was high, life spans were short, and everyday existence was hardscrabble. In the modern secular world, skepticism has replaced faith as the default psychology of countless people, so the issue has changed. Now it is about appearance versus reality. As a Zen saying puts it, "To the awakened mind, there is no such thing as birth or death, only the constant unfolding of the eternal now." Mysticism has faded in favor of metaphysics.

This insight provides a goal that doesn't have to wait for death in order to settle what is real and what is illusion. The awakened life is available here and now—we are moving toward it in these sutras. But it would be unfortunate to exclude the rational mind, which after all is the modern standard of proof. Direct, effortless knowing is the highest form of knowledge; nothing can change that. It would be helpful, though, if the rational mind stopped putting up such strong resistance, particularly when that resistance is irrational.

Set aside questions of faith and belief. Best estimates tell us that only 25 percent of Americans don't believe in Heaven and Hell, which shows how stubbornly tradition hangs on in the collective consciousness. Rationally, since science has reached no consensus on the afterlife, any opinion pro or con isn't based on evidence. But there's another way to arrive at an answer—the path of gyana, the path of direct knowing that this book is based on.

Gyana points to awareness and asks, "What can you reduce it to that is more basic?" Water, ice, and steam can be reduced to H_2O. Buddhism can be reduced to the Four Noble Truths and the Eightfold Path. Music can be reduced to scales and chords. But consciousness is irreducible. It is only itself. Nothing lies behind it as a cause or an antecedent. There are analogies to this all around us. Prior to time appearing at the instant of the Big Bang, there was no time, but this means that there was nothing "before" time, since *before* needs time in order to have any meaning. Space also appeared during the Big Bang, which means that the Big Bang had no location—location is a concept that has no meaning without space, which didn't exist yet.

To illustrate this further, imagine that you are the CEO of Universe Creation, Inc., and a client comes to you saying, "Please build me a universe with time and space in it. By the way, what will you build them from?" You won't have an answer. The human brain, being a construct of time and space, can't conceive of any "stuff" that precedes time and space. We don't have to get cosmic about it. How do you build wetness? It is only itself. Without it, you have dryness, but it makes no sense to say that wetness is made from dryness.

However, consciousness is even more irreducible. If a client came to the source, saying, "I'd like a universe with love in it. By the way, what are you going to build love from?" the answer from pure consciousness would be "From myself." The same answer would apply to every subjective quality like curiosity, compassion, insight, or epiphany. It's only logical. If there's nothing that precedes consciousness as its cause, then consciousness doesn't have a separate toolbox that it can reach into. Only itself exists; therefore, it has no choice but to create everything from itself.

Subjective qualities like love and compassion are easier to grasp because we experience them "in here," but pure consciousness has no external toolbox or instruction manual for time, space, matter, and energy "out there." If a client asks the source where time, space, matter, and energy come from, "From myself" still is the only logical answer. The rational mind can relax and stop feeling that it is being dragged against its will into unreason and mysticism.

Finally, a client might appear, saying, "I want a universe with human beings in it. By the way, what are you going to make them from?" There is still no other answer besides "From myself," which is why the fact that consciousness has no origin story means that you don't, either. Your existence arises from the irreducible foundation of consciousness itself.

Finding Your Wisdom

SKY MEDITATION

THERE ARE ANCIENT INDIAN MEDITATIONS, PARTICULARLY in the Shiva tradition of Kashmir, that use the sky as a portal to unbounded consciousness. A simple practice consists of lying on your back and gazing softly at a clear blue sky. (Preferably you are in an open space where the sky fills your entire field of vision.) Contemplate the sky as a symbol of the boundless field of creation.

Now shut your eyes. An afterimage of the sky will remain on your retina. Imagine that this "inner sky" is your version of the same vast, unbounded creation.

Softly open and close your eyes, letting the inner and outer sky merge. See the boundless expanse of creation as being inside and outside at the same time, a single creation with no boundary to separate anything.

Finally, with eyes closed, observe any thoughts that cross your mind. Say to yourself, "These thoughts come and go like clouds across a blue sky. They appear and disappear, but the sky remains unchanged." This is the field of pure consciousness that has no origin, because it is absolute wholeness.

Waking up from your identity as a person Brings total freedom

·

ACH OF US THINKS OF OURSELVES AS A PERSON. BEING A PER-
son is the basis of what we call personality, and personality is entirely
wrapped up in your life story. By their nature, stories have twists and
turns, so they aren't permanent. They are provisional; in other words,
good enough for the moment but subject to change.

This setup of being a fixed person, like a lighthouse immune from
the storm, which seems quite normal, has a built-in contradiction,
however. The person isn't above the storm. Invisibly, your identity
adapts to how your story is unfolding. The feeling of being like a
lighthouse is deceptive. Far from being permanent, your identity is
provisional. You maintain the illusion of being steadily, reliably, consistently yourself, and for what? To avoid the insecurity of being un-
moored. Better the illusion of being permanent than standing up to
the prospect of impermanence—no one wants to be a scrap of news-
paper being blown down the street by the next wind.

But these are imagined threats. You have been provisional all your
life, and learning how to adapt and change has been a major strength.
It's a fantasy to believe that being immovable and rock solid can
spare anyone from accidents, natural disasters, disease, failure, loss,
change of fortune, or any other form of pain and suffering. The issue
is not how to be saved from bad things but how to adapt and survive

them. Coming to terms with that reality is so difficult that most people don't—they hope that bad things will happen to other people and not to them. They push their deepest fears out of sight. They cling to the illusion that, as a person, they can keep identifying with a stable self that is unaffected by harsh realities.

The mental defenses we construct to protect our sense of self would make perfect sense if there wasn't any alternative, but there is. When you wake up, you stop identifying with the person—with its provisional, changing identity; its stories, skewed perceptions, confusing experiences; birth and death itself. All those issues arise from the illusion of being a person. From the viewpoint of your true nature, the person is just a phenomenon like any other, an experience whose nature is transient. The world is a constant parade of phenomena, and you don't automatically identify with them. A cloud, a school bus, pedestrians waiting at the crosswalk, passing stories in the news, another uprising in a country you can't locate on a map—none of these affects you as a person.

The difference is in what you do identify with. They are the things that leave karmic impressions of memory. Consider fear. If you go to a horror movie, fear is entertainment. If you have a nightmare, fear is a feeling that vanishes when you wake up. Very different is the fear that symptoms of a cold could be COVID or worse. Any fear that grips you is one that you identify with. (I have a friend whose mother called him anytime she saw a plane crash in the news, just to reassure herself that he wasn't on it. This was a fear she strongly identified with.)

THE ONLY SOLUTION IS to get free of the machinery that automatically creates a person. Do that, and there is no fear, no separation, no birth, and no death. They are all phenomena you don't have to identify with.

Awareness is free of phenomena, just as the bed of the ocean is free of the waves on its surface. At any moment when you are disturbed or distressed by an experience, remind yourself, "I am the awareness in which this is a passing event." In a calm, quiet moment of reflection, look around you and say to yourself, "I am aware, here and now. Everything I see is just the passing scenery."

Seeing yourself as a person is a deeply ingrained habit, but awareness offers a vision of total freedom. Getting there is a process, but every step of awakening brings you closer.

Finding Your Wisdom

FREEDOM NOW

NO MATTER WHAT KIND OF A BIND YOU GET YOURSELF into, your awareness enjoys total freedom. *Total* in this case means "perpetual, permanent, everlasting, boundless, and unconditional." Awareness doesn't have to do anything to achieve unconditional freedom—by its very nature it is free. What this means is that the state of awareness we take to be normal is actually abnormal. Seeing yourself as a person, you have adapted to an abnormal state without consciously deciding to make such a choice.

Your provisional self—call it the person, ego, personality, or simply "I"—has no right to keep your awareness bound up in this way. You have expended untold time and effort building up this person you carry around as an invisible weight. Just remember that no matter how much effort it takes to lift a weight, it takes close to no effort to drop it.

Here's an exercise that will free you right now.

EXERCISE

Sit quietly and focus on your mind. You have no idea what your next thought will be. It could be momentous or insignificant, a breakthrough, or the repetition of old routine thoughts. Therefore, you have no stable, reliable relationship with your mind. You are free to have no attitude toward it—positive or negative. You are free to say, "I am not my thoughts."

Now focus on time. You don't know what the future will bring. Things could go wrong or right. Predictable events will be mixed with random ones. Therefore, you have no stable, reliable relationship with the future. You are free to say, "I am not my future."

Finally, think of karma. Karma is a pattern of events that will happen out of the blue, seemingly without a cause. Karma causes us to say, "Why me?" It's a question that applies to good fortune as well as misfortune. You have no control over karma; therefore, you have no stable or reliable relationship to external events. You are free to have no attitude to the external world—positive or negative. You are free to say, "I am not the world around me."

It took quite a few words to explain this exercise, but the simple outcome is "I am not my thoughts. I am not my future. I am not the world around me." These are the realizations that free you from the imprisonment of the person. Awareness is stating what is, nothing more.

We are drawn to freedom, But we also fear it

•

ONE RULE ABOUT THE AWAKENED LIFE, AND EXPANDED awareness generally, is that you have to agree to it. Nothing changes against your will. You aren't forced to be more loving or creative. If you cling to the waking dream, that's your choice. It's the choice that countless people make, even when they read about everything good that comes with awakening.

One problem is that most people have little or no idea about the things we've been talking about: pure consciousness, the source, infinite possibilities, Maya. You have to go out of your way to show interest in questions that society totally ignores.

But let's say that the clouds clear, and someone is offered the prospect of complete freedom from illusion. In that freedom, truth and reality merge and can never be separated. The noted Indian spiritual teacher J. Krishnamurti called this "the first and last freedom," which combines the beginning and end of the spiritual path into one step: directly perceiving your own conditioning and at that moment being liberated from it. Krishnamurti wrote, "It is only when the mind is free from the old that it meets everything anew, and in that there is joy."

Holding out such a promise, wouldn't people choose to be free? Here is where the difficulty lies. We are naturally drawn to freedom, but we also fear it. The question of choice is cloudy. Most of us feel that we were dropped into the world we accept as real; no one gave us a choice. Likewise, even when we are told that our situation is like a prisoner who doesn't realize that his jail cell isn't locked, what does it mean to walk out of the cell? Maya makes the world a livable place, adapted to the human nervous system. You can't choose to walk away from your nervous system.

Plato's Allegory of the Cave provides a vivid example. Imagine prisoners who have been chained in a dark cave their entire lives, seeing only shadows cast on the wall. To them, the shadows are reality. Now imagine that one prisoner is freed and steps out into the light. At first, the light is blinding, and the outside world seems incomprehensible. But as his eyes adjust, the prisoner begins to see things as they truly are. The journey out of the cave mirrors the process of freeing oneself from illusion. It also highlights why so many hesitate—freedom can be disorienting and bewildering at first.

The very prospect of abandoning the darkness has been known to induce anxiety, the fear of freedom that the desire for freedom doesn't erase. In spiritual traditions, especially Catholicism, this inner conflict is called the dark night of the soul. It's the fear of losing what you thought you were. It's the fear of losing what you think is your identity. But all identity is provisional except for "I am," which arises from your source. Ultimately, whenever the dark night of the soul creates despair, the same fear is expressing itself: the fear of losing one's provisional identity. This is yet another result of thinking that "I" is a fixed object worth holding on to, like a diamond or a bar of gold. That act of holding on is the root of desperation at the prospect of freedom, which involves letting go.

To be aware of the fear of freedom is actually the beginning of freedom. In some ways, there is no other step to take. If you commit to letting go, you aren't stepping out of the waking dream. Your ego-personality is having a passing thought. Awareness isn't a thought. That is precisely what is freeing about it. If you find yourself futilely going on a new diet, reading about miraculous longevity regimens, suffering over the aging process, or worrying that you are losing out to competition at work, such preoccupations are resistance to being aware. You are fighting against or denying your fear. You are grasping at straws when a single moment of genuine self-awareness can free you of the whole tangled mess.

A repeated theme in awakening is that you start to live from the level of solution, rather than being mired in the level of the problem. Any worry that you are obsessed with or fixated on is at the level of the problem. You somehow believe that if you keep obsessing long and hard enough, a solution will appear. With clear sight, you realize that this won't happen. The same applies to our conflicted feelings about freedom. Dwelling on the conflict produces no new results, no answers, and ultimately no freedom. Clinging to a false identity is how we mire ourselves at the level of the problem. Becoming aware of awareness reveals that "I am" is the only true self, an imperishable identity merged into the very nature of consciousness.

Finding Your Wisdom

A TASTE OF FREEDOM

THE LIBERATION THAT HAPPENS "IN HERE" ISN'T THE same as other, more familiar kinds of freedom, such as religious and political freedom, freedom of speech, and freedom from slavery. Those liberties exist in the relative world, while inner liberation aspires to be total or absolute freedom. The difference is that no circumstances can alter absolute freedom; no one can take it away from you.

If that is the acid test, then total freedom can't be achieved in the relative world, which is dominated by change. There are other aspects of total freedom that are important. It doesn't apply to your ego or personality, because total freedom isn't something you can think or talk about. You can't compare yourself with someone else who isn't free. There are no external signs, no behavior or way of talking that announces, "I am totally free."

The only condition that meets these tests is a state of awareness that is awake and living close to the source. In other words, it is part of your being to be free. Once you realize this, choice becomes irrelevant, like choosing whether to breathe or to have your DNA divide to produce new cells. The closest approximation to total freedom is "I am," but even that falls short, since words are thoughts, and freedom isn't achieved by thinking about it.

Here is a simple exercise to give you a taste of total freedom using the intuition that bypasses thinking and words, relying on pure knowing instead.

EXERCISE

Sit quietly in a dim or dark room so that when you close your eyes, your field of vision isn't bright. Now imagine that the room is beginning to be filled with white light. See it fill up until you are surrounded only by light—the contents and walls of the room have disappeared.

See the light coming into your body from all directions until it gently makes your body disappear. Your faintest outline fades away. Now you are sitting in a field of white light. Let yourself rest there for a moment, quietly and calmly. This is the simple state of "I am" without interference from the ego or the mind.

To live fully, live in the now, For now is infinite and eternal

·

IT'S A STRANGE ASPECT OF EVERYDAY LIFE THAT WE AVOID WHAT is happening now, in the present moment. There is deep spiritual significance hidden in this statement. The now is disguised by our habit of looking ahead or behind, anticipating the future and reliving the past. In doing so, we miss the real world, which is always here and now. In spiritual terms, now is everything. By avoiding the now, we plunge into illusion.

The hidden meaning of now—the reality that presents itself at every instant—was divine as expressed by the medieval mystic Meister Eckhart. "God is creating the entire universe, fully and totally in this present now. Everything God created—God creates now all at once." Substitute the words *pure consciousness* for God, and the essence remains the same. What makes creation eternal is that it happens now.

This goes far beyond the popular notion of being present. We say things like, "You're not present right now" or "Sorry, I was having a hard time being present." But these acknowledgments do little to break our habit of looking behind and ahead. We need to go deeper into what *now* means.

On the surface, now is a point in time. The annual New York City Marathon begins at 8:00 a.m., a specific point in time for the select professional runners. But the instant the starter's gun goes off, now has vanished into the past. The same is true if you simply think or say the word *now*. As soon as it registers in your brain the thought or word has fled.

Therefore, being in the now is much trickier than our idea of present-moment awareness. All experience has fled into the past the instant the present moment happens, moving from reality to memory. This isn't the fault of the human nervous system. Every cell in your body, including your brain, operates strictly in the present. Thousands of processes—combining proteins, taking in nutrients and dispelling wastes, respiration, cell division and repair—take place with perfect organization in the now. If you call up a memory of your first kiss or your tenth birthday party, the impression of revisiting the past is a mental illusion. The brain cells that generate the memory fire in the present because life itself takes place now and only now. Hence the significance of Rumi's words: "Let life live through you."

We need such advice because letting life live through us is exactly what we're not doing. It turns out that there's a problem with defining now as a point in time. Now doesn't actually have a duration. You can't measure it with a stopwatch or even an atomic clock. Consider a string. Someone tells you to divide the string in two by marking a point halfway between both ends. That's easy enough, and there's no difficulty if you are asked to divide the string into 10, 100, or 1 million equal parts. Mathematically, you can divide the string into infinite points, because a point, as mathematicians define it, has no length. Likewise, now has no duration, so you can technically put a million points inside one second, or infinite points.

Suddenly, the whole picture is changing. If now has no duration, it isn't long or short. You can fit something very small into it, like noticing a leaf the instant it falls from a tree, or something very large, like contemplating thousands of galaxies in one image from the Hubble Telescope. Yet even this doesn't go far enough. Now isn't about size or numbers. Now is a point in awareness. In the teachings of Yoga, the sharpest, clearest state of alertness is known as one-pointed awareness (*ekagrata* in Sanskrit). When you have one-pointed awareness, you are in the now. For example, think of a painter fully immersed in her work, each brushstroke guided by total focus. In that moment, the past and the future fade away. In terms of awakening, one-pointedness doesn't need anything outside itself to focus on. Now is a steady state of awareness.

Traditionally, you will see one-pointedness associated with meditation as highly concentrated attention, which implies long effort and training. We can set that aside for the moment, because the emphasis needs to be on wakefulness as a natural state of awareness, not the product of work and discipline. The revered modern spiritual teacher Nisargadatta Maharaj makes this point very clearly: "The feeling is primarily of being present and aware. Wherever you go, the sense of here and now you carry with you all the time. It means that you are independent of space and time, that space and time are in you, not you in them."

Once you understand that now is eternal—independent of time and space—an essential truth dawns: You are not in time and space, either, not the essential you that always lives in the now. It's important not to pigeonhole this realization to India. From the Christian mystical tradition in medieval Europe, Meister Eckhart echoes centuries of wisdom when he writes, "There is within the soul a power which is uncreated and uncreatable; this power is the same as God."

This is a perfect example of how Gyan Yoga, the Yoga of knowingness, helps to liberate us by bringing a hidden truth to light.

You will never see the simple word *now* in the same light again.

Finding Your Wisdom

A COSMIC CONSPIRACY

THE REALIZATION THAT NOW ISN'T IN TIME AND SPACE leads to many implications. Here's one that applies personally: The whole universe conspires to bring about the present moment. This is already an accepted fact in quantum physics, made popular by the phrase "When an electron vibrates, the universe shakes." In other words, no particle can move without sending a ripple through the quantum field.

Every experience you've ever had sent ripples through the field of pure consciousness. The difference from physics— a huge difference—is that the field knows what is happening. The ripple is a ripple of understanding, and in return, the next instant of now brings a reaction from the field.

In other words, everything in creation is conspiring to bring about the present moment. Reality is now and now and now and now, eternally. Let a stray beam of sunlight or starlight fall on your eye. The photons that carry the light are 18 billion years old and also present right now. Reflect on the composition of your body. There are traces of copper, zinc, and iodine in your physical makeup. These elements exist on Earth because a supernova exploded somewhere in the universe, creating inter-stellar dust that eventually came to this planet—another con-nection to the now that is billions of years old at the same time. It's only a little harder to connect now and the infinite.

Here is a simple exercise: Let your mind wander and notice your next thought. Before and after the thought was a silent gap. That gap consists of pure awareness. You experience this pure awareness now, but its source is the wholeness of aware-ness, which is eternal and infinite.

To take this a step further, say to yourself, "I was not born in space and time. They are born 'in here,' in my awareness, which can't be measured in time or space."

You are at the very center of creation, Here and now

·

BECAUSE YOU ARE ALIVE, AWARE, AND INTELLIGENT, YOU PLAY a crucial role in creating the reality around you. The present moment has no content without you to perceive and interpret it. Even when you filter the present moment through memory of the past or anticipation of the future, you can't entirely abandon it. You aren't a passive observer plopped into the world like a movie camera dropped onto a busy city street, recording the day's events. You are the source observing itself through the eyes of a co-creator—your awareness plays an active role.

There's a key phrase in the Bhagavad Gita where Krishna declares, "Curving back on myself, I create again and again." This is the source speaking, indicating that creation is a continuous process, contradicting the Book of Genesis, where creation ends after seven days, and also the Big Bang, where creation took place once and for all 13.8 billion years ago. In the case of the Big Bang, once and for all applies to matter and energy, which cannot be created or destroyed once they appear, only transformed. They are free to evolve into atoms, molecules, stars, galaxies, and human DNA. (The discovery of black holes makes the impossibility of destroying matter and energy very wobbly, however.)

None of this would seem to include you, much less does the physical universe need you as co-creator. That role is undertaken, not physically, but in consciousness. Even before awakening, your awareness colors and transforms your reality, making you an active co-creator in the world. The difference once awakening happens is that your role becomes much deeper and more fundamental. You expand your role as a co-creator in only one way: by reaching higher states of consciousness. Years ago, I read that enlightened masters "precipitate reality onto the Earth."

Only later did I realize that this is a central doctrine of Buddhism. The Buddha possessed a "truth body," meaning that he had every attribute of pure consciousness. A second teaching holds that all sentient creatures have "Buddha nature," which gives them the potential to reach that same level of truth. In this way, the absolute reality of pure consciousness is kept alive on Earth.

If a fully conscious person is like a clear, wide channel for consciousness to flow through, everyone, no matter what their state of awareness might be, is also a channel. It might be a narrow channel, a soda straw compared with a water main, but it must exist for each of us to be alive, aware, and intelligent.

What makes your role active instead of passive is the transformations you create, which are radical and totally necessary. As you channel pure consciousness, you are working with raw ore, so to speak. The source is timeless and formless. Once creative intelligence passes through you, however, all the qualities of consciousness emerge in the world. Pure consciousness isn't hot or cold, soft or hard, smooth or rough, bright or dim, and so on. Once the raw ore is channeled through you, any quality your nervous system can register is free to appear. Just as only awareness is aware, only awareness can perceive these qualities. It's a hard concept to grasp when all of us have been raised on the physical world as the be-all and end-all. How is it possible that granite isn't hard, gold doesn't glitter, and a red apple has no color without us? Because redness needs a human to make it red. All light is colorless in Nature; frequencies and vibrations are matters of mathematics, not experience. Any quality you can name needs a source in consciousness. The hardness of granite isn't dependent on human awareness the way colors, sounds, touch, taste, and smell are.

They don't exist outside us, although some equivalent is present, of course, in various higher life-forms. The hardness of granite demands a worldview where the source takes on the job of creating every quality in the human world, including the ones we have no personal control over.

All of those qualities are transformed from pure consciousness. As for your role, imagine yourself a prism for a moment. As white light passes through you, your physical makeup is transformed into rays of colors. Diversity emerges from oneness.

The view is breathtaking from here. Awareness creates all transformations, making each quality fit into the tapestry of the human world. You and I personally don't have to re-create the tapestry. It's a legacy, held in place by collective consciousness from generation to generation. Yet the central point remains. It took the evolution of human consciousness, starting from the origin of life 4 billion years ago, to creatively weave the tapestry, using the transformational power of awareness.

Finding Your Wisdom

RECOGNIZE THIS?

IF YOU ASK, "HOW DO WE KNOW THAT THE WORLD EXISTS?" a philosopher's eyes will brighten, because you've hit on a hugely important question. The way in which we perceive or know anything is cognition. I cognize you when you walk into a room, but I probably don't cognize a single baby spider in the corner.

You might wonder why I didn't say that I *recognize* you when you walk into the room, but to say the word *recognize* adds a second, highly personal act. To "re-cognize" is to know or perceive again. Imagine trying to tell the color of any object—a shoe, a piece of cloth, or a vase—in a darkened room. The retina doesn't perceive color in very dim light, but as you steadily brighten the room, you will recognize that the shoe is brown, the cloth bright red, the vase sky blue. You turned raw perception into recognition.

This has been an abstract description, I know, but it is vitally important to see that everything in the world requires an act of recognition. In that act, you add your awareness and any quality you bring with it. Consider two photos—one of someone you love and the other of someone else you strongly dislike. When you recognize the faces, you won't add the same emotional quality, even if the two photos are of identical twins—once you know which photo is which, the same love or animosity kicks in, even though your eye perceives identical images.

Recognition draws from a host of things: memory, emotion, expectations, and private associations. You might have experienced a neighborhood house of horrors on Halloween where children wander around in the dark. They might be asked to plunge their hands into a bowl of human brains—actually a bowl of cold wet spaghetti—and the expectation creates a squeal of momentary horror.

Yet out of that example, we can see the treachery of recognition, which is never pure cognition. Cognition depends upon an open path between pure consciousness and your awareness. There is no blockage or interference. Therefore, the transformation that creates the world around us is open, fresh, new, and filled with presence. Recognition sacrifices those qualities, to which we can also add bliss.

There is no specific exercise here. Just notice the next time an experience feels joyful and new to you. Pause for a moment. See in that joy and freshness that you are a co-creator of reality with the source. Notice how natural and effortless this is. Once you see the value in direct cognition, even the most familiar face or everyday experience can change. Instead of being a reflection you recognize from the past, it can be a moment of now.

Creation is absolute. It defeats chaos, disorder, and decay.

•

CREATION ISN'T THE OPPOSITE OF DESTRUCTION. CREATION is absolute: At the source, it has no opposite and therefore no opposition. If you go by appearances, however, destruction looks like it has the upper hand. On Earth all living things are temporary, eventually giving in to physical decay. In basic physics, it is taught that entropy is a law that cannot be overcome. Entropy is defined as the tendency of order to give way to disorder as heat dissipates the way the body after death turns cold, stars burn out, and ice cubes melt in the sun.

Maya rules appearances, but it's a mistake to assume that an appearance is always shallow. This might apply to someone who appears to be friendly but is masking darker feelings; however, in spiritual terms the whole world is perceived as an appearance. Therefore, Maya is as complex as Nature itself. Every page of every volume in a medical library testifies to the complexity of the waking dream. The only way to expose the dream is by realizing that consciousness can transform itself into physical objects. Physicality is the last stop on the journey from the source.

It sounds absurd to say that a leg bone is conscious—why not a rock or the carbon monoxide emitted by a diesel truck? The last stop on the journey from the source isn't self-consciousness—bones, rocks, and carbon monoxide aren't possessed of a mind. But they don't escape the net cast by consciousness, which is all-inclusive. Your bones, blood, liver, and all other tissues participate in the consciousness that creates and maintains the human body. The physical tissue of the brain is just as mindless as bone tissue, but the expression of consciousness is different between the two. Awareness expresses as thought in the brain; it expresses in the enormously complex life of a bone cell, only silently.

The fact that consciousness is all-embracing makes it absolute. Chaos, disorder, and decay are not all-embracing. They are stages in the whole process of creation. Your last thought had to fade away to nothing in order for you to have your next thought. Every cell is programmed to die in order to make way for new cells. Supernovae exploded in spectacular acts of annihilation so that the interstellar dust they created could become an essential part of life on Earth.

Entropy itself must bow to consciousness. That's not textbook physics, but cosmologists are steadily coming to terms with the reality that consciousness is innate in the universe. There is no physical explanation for how mind can be created from physical stuff, which makes it inevitable that consciousness, like matter and energy, can't be created or destroyed, only transformed. The stumbling block that remains is still huge. A younger generation of tolerant physicists is willing to accept ideas like "We live in a conscious universe" or "Matter contains proto-consciousness, an early stage before consciousness emerged."

Such statements still tend to put matter before mind. Seen clearly, it is just as hard to inject awareness into atoms and molecules as it is to create mind out of atoms and molecules. When and how was this done? No one has an answer. There's a stubborn disbelief that creation isn't physical in the first place. As viewed from the source, consciousness turns itself into the created universe, along with every physical object like the human body and brain.

Demoting matter elevates awareness. That has been part of a historical pattern that rocks like a seesaw. In an age of faith, God transcends the physical world, placing divine awareness above everything. In the scientific age, nothing transcends matter, making it difficult even to admit that mind exists—neuroscience considers mind a by-product of brain activity, the way a bonfire gives off heat and smoke as by-products. But in everyday life the mind has no difficulty moving matter. Your brain chemistry is completely altered by hearing someone say "I love you," and the cascade of hormones triggered merely by words can deeply affect you for an entire relationship, only to be altered just as radically by hearing the words "I don't love you anymore."

Creation, to put it as succinctly as possible, is the mover behind everything. In the state of separation, all we can observe is appearances. If the solid, tangible thing-ness of physical objects no longer convinces you, Maya is indifferent. It remains in charge of physical creation regardless of anyone's beliefs, perceptions, and interpretations. A scientist as great as Isacc Newton was a fundamentalist Christian, harboring a firm belief that the Old Testament was a factual historical record, but this conviction had no impact on Newton's grasp of physics.

As far as appearances go, creation is counterbalanced by destruction, as if in a war for domination. Hinduism depicts the physical world driven by three forces named as gods—Brahma the god of creation, Vishnu the god of maintenance, and Shiva the god of destruction. They can be taken literally without mythical connotations, since every physical phenomenon is created, lasts for a while, and is then destroyed by dismantling it into its atomic and subatomic building blocks.

As far as the mechanics go, this cycle is indisputable. But pause to consider why creation, maintenance, and destruction were given divine status—because they are not blind forces but conscious and self-organized. Reducing Nature to a vast contraption of moving mechanical parts captures the appearance of the cosmos but not its very essence. In baseball, an X-ray of the muscles in a pitcher's throwing arm captures a mechanical motion while missing entirely the art and skill of pitching. Take away their divine names, and the underlying processes symbolized by Brahma, Vishnu, and Shiva are still conscious, transcending the appearance that entropy is in charge.

If entropy held sway, then destruction, death, and decay would be elevated to a position they don't deserve. Destruction is never the last word in Nature; no mass extinction is ever a total extinction. (It's fascinating to read that current findings supported by thousands of fossils date birds back at least 90 million years, meaning they flew in the age of dinosaurs and managed to survive the mass extinction of dinosaurs 65 million years ago. There are estimated to have been thousands of species of primordial birds. Only small ground birds survived the catastrophic meteor collision. With these modest survivors evolution started over, and now we are surrounded by eleven thousand replacement species of birds—their second coming.) Creation wouldn't defeat chaos, disorder, and decay if the mechanics set up by Maya operated blindly. Full awakening reveals the reality that creation is absolute. Thanks to this, human creativity in its essence enjoys the same status.

Finding Your Wisdom

PREPARING FOR "AHA"

P EOPLE HAVE FOUND THEIR LIVES CHANGED BY TRANS-formative moments when something hidden is revealed, insight replaces confusion, and certainty erases doubt. Ideally, we should be open to them anytime. The more comfortable you are with trusting your insights and intuition, the more likely that "aha" moments will appear.

The most common "aha" moment occurs when a solution suddenly emerges to a problem that has stubbornly resisted answers. You are stuck with a task at work, in research, in some creative activity where you feel blocked, or in an unsettled relationship. In such situations the habit of recognition works against you, because you rely on the futile hope that repeatedly juggling familiar thoughts over and over will somehow lead to a new solution. What you need instead is a cognition, that is, a direct understanding of the answer.

To prepare for an "aha" experience, begin by not putting up obstacles. These belong in the category of focusing on the level of the problem instead of the level of the solution. Getting stuck at the level of the problem involves feeling stressed and overburdened, inner confusion, conflicting answers, overthinking, and obsessive thinking. Removing these obstacles involves the opposite: feeling relaxed, in control, mentally calm, and free of overthinking.

To clear these obstacles, cultivate a sense of relaxation, mental calmness, and freedom from overthinking. When you notice yourself slipping into stress or mental overload, take a break. Step away from the problem and find something else that quiets the mind, like taking a walk, meditating, or doing light exercise. You want to clear a mental space where insights can naturally arise.

This isn't idle time—something important is happening. By stepping back, you are opening a channel to your source. A shift in attitude can help here: Trust that the right solution exists in deeper awareness. Avoid placing pressure on yourself to find the answer as an isolated individual. Place your trust in simple awareness, which is fully capable of coming up with creative answers in everyday life. Many of the most successful people have a secret: They know how to get out of their own way.

Finally, being creative at something you love opens the flow of creative intelligence in general. We're not talking only about artists and musicians with gifts. Anyone can experience the creative state by finding a hobby, craft, or activity that brings focus, absorption, and pleasure. When you are in the creative state, and love what you are doing, you will find yourself simultaneously relaxed and aware. This is the perfect stage setting for an "aha" experience.

Use memory
Without letting it use you

·

Waking up—in other words, being fully conscious—changes your entire relationship to memory. You leave behind a host of personal memories that define you as separate and isolated. They are the memories of the story that you created around yourself in the waking dream. A new use of memory dawns, in which you need no story or separate identity; you remember that you are being created at every moment by the flow of pure awareness.

Awakening is therefore a forgetting and a remembering at the same time. There's a parallel in everyday life going back to childhood development. When you learned to talk, you forgot what it was like when speech was just random sounds. Learning the alphabet led you to forget what it was like to see letters as indecipherable marks on the page.

Memory is infinitely useful. A medical school library is hardly large enough to describe the processes your cells remember to perform every minute you are alive. You take for granted that you've handed over the responsibility for remaining alive to your brain as coordinator of the autonomic (or involuntary) nervous system. You handed over much more without a second thought. Muscle memory retains every physical skill without having to be relearned every time you hit a tennis ball or flip a pancake. Specific areas of the brain are associated with the minutiae of memory—for example, one aspect of memory allows you to recognize a familiar house on sight, but another small cluster of cells allows you to recognize it as your house and not someone else's.

We could go on and build a case for Maya and the entire waking dream being a product of memory. Maya is the transformation station, you might say, where formless pure consciousness acquires form. Once a form is set in place, whether it is a sodium atom, the Andromeda nebula, or a brain cell, memory keeps that form intact. (The brain, itself part of the waking dream, doesn't have a privileged position on its own. It conforms to what Maya creates.)

Yet within this framework there is a shadow zone where the possibility of waking up exists. This possibility was left open for a very simple reason. Pure consciousness overrides all appearances. Its reality supersedes anything that Maya has control over. Maya can't set absolute rules that run mind, body, brain, and universe as its playthings. Maya is a user. We are being used as pieces in a grand design, but consciousness never fails to recognize itself, the ultimate act of remembering.

Your mind and body are products of memory, and there's no denying memory's usefulness. But you can't keep playing by Maya's rules and expect to free yourself. The path to awakening requires you to forget and remember at the same time. What dawns somewhere along the path is that the source can be trusted. We have handed over responsibility for the day-to-day operation of the body and mind. It takes a flow of creative intelligence for those operations to work seamlessly. What else in our lives can be handed over or surrendered?

That's the question you need to ask every day because you can't hand over responsibility for things you cling to. Your grip must ease. A knowing voice will quietly let you know that some aspect of worry, habit, old traumas, automatic reactions, resentments, envy, hostility, and depression can be released because it is time. That voice is the part of you connected to your source and, as you remember it, you can forget the part of you that clings to the past and worries about the future so desperately. The two things—forgetting and remembering—occur simultaneously, and neither requires effort. At every step your motto should be, "I use memory. I do not allow memory to use me."

Finding Your Wisdom

SPIRITUAL FORGETTING

THE PROSPECT OF FORGETTING RAISES GRIM THOUGHTS about aging, memory loss, and dementia. Within such a pessimistic, anxious scheme, the spiritual side of forgetting is lost. It is only regained when you consider that waking up in the morning clears your memory of the night's dreams, either immediately or in a short time. The vanished dream is forgotten without anxiety, and if it was a bad dream, you are happy to forget it.

Spiritual forgetting is optimistic, as Lao Tzu declares: "When I let go of what I am, I become what I might be." It's all right to take a tentative attitude; this is unknown territory for almost everyone. A good practice centers on repetitive thoughts. When you have any kind of discouraging or judgmental thought, see it as the past trying to intrude where it isn't wanted. Address your mind by saying, "I've heard this same thought over and over again. I don't need it anymore." Another option when such thoughts crop up is to address the thought directly, saying, "I've listened to you for a long time. I don't need the message repeated."

In today's troubled landscape, happiness is seen as fragile, elusive, and temporary at best. This attitude presupposes that the mind's normal state isn't happy, which is the opposite of spiritual forgetting, where you are reconnecting with a permanent state, not just of happiness, but also of joy, bliss, love, discovery, and every other spiritual value. When you have a glimpse of these experiences, pause and think, "I'm seeing the real me. I'm remembering why I exist."

What I've outlined here is the meshing of forgetting and remembering that this sutra is all about. Any moment of re-connection with your source is an act of remembering; any moment when you detach yourself from old, outworn thinking is an act of spiritual forgetting.

You experience awakening, Your brain doesn't

Y OUR BRAIN IS A PHYSICAL OBJECT, AND ALL PHYSICAL OBJECTS exist in the waking dream. This simple bit of logic demotes the brain, shattering any claim that the brain is thinking, feeling, or doing anything else that requires awareness. If it isn't thinking, what is your brain doing? It is mirroring your consciousness. To give an analogy, as I type words on my keyboard, they appear on the computer monitor. I see a mirror of what my mind is doing. The keyboard didn't think up the words in this sentence; the monitor has no experience of what words mean.

Likewise, you see mental images the way you see images on a computer monitor, as a reflection of what your consciousness is doing. People know this intuitively, which is why we say, "I need to speak to customer service" or "I want new shoes" instead of "My brain needs to speak to customer service" or "My brain wants new shoes."

As a physical object, the brain can be treated like any other bodily organ. An awakened perception doesn't negate the value of brain scans like an fMRI, brain surgery, antidepressants, and tranquilizers—as we've seen, Maya is set up so that the physical universe fulfills our human needs. But when a surgeon is removing a brain tumor or a psychiatrist prescribes Prozac, consciousness isn't being treated.

Because the brain isn't the mind, it can't wake up. It provides an image, in brain waves and the activation of specific brain regions, of waking up, which is useful for research into what higher states of consciousness look like from the outside. The most perfect physical measurements are still part of the waking dream, no matter how realistic the imaging might be. You watch yourself in the mirror brushing your teeth, and every single gesture is perfectly reflected, but you'd never imagine that your reflection is brushing its teeth.

It is quite amazing how the brain's quadrillion connections can register activity not just on the cellular level but all the way down to the quantum field. Yet even here the brain isn't particularly special. The world outside your window also operates down to the quantum level with perfect coordination. Maya runs the world and your brain with the same precision, which plays a crucial part in awakening.

In the Indian tradition, the physical body is a vehicle that conveys you on the spiritual journey, like a rowboat carrying you to a far shore (the Sanskrit term is *vāhana*). A vehicle is needed because the spiritual journey takes place within the physical world. *Vāhana* takes you to spiritual experiences, but your brain and body don't know what is happening; only your awareness does. Think of this as driving your car on vacation. It gets you to your destination, but it wouldn't make sense to say that your car is noticing the scenery along the way.

What makes awakening such a thrilling prospect is that you get to use Maya's rules subversively—the illusion is the vehicle for escaping the illusion. This act of defiance is the very definition of freedom. Maya's rules are looser than you imagine. There are all kinds of loopholes—exceptions, anomalies, and interruptions—once you start looking.

Out of millions of five-year-olds, a few will be able to play the violin or piano with advanced ability. That defies Maya's rule that every child's brain develops by fixed stages, beginning with the most rudimentary physical abilities, like holding a cup of juice in your hands without spilling it. Math prodigies at the same young age can tell you the square root of a six-digit number almost as soon as they hear the number. They don't think through ordinary methods to arrive at the answer (which normally requires an advanced computer program). The answer is just there for the asking. So-called calendar savants do the same when asked what day of the week any date in history falls upon.

These feats defy cause and effect, which would appear to be one of Maya's unbreakable rules. Linear thinking isn't involved. Such phenomena provide clues about what consciousness can do when it bypasses all conventional explanations. Once you stop believing that the rules of everyday existence aren't ironclad, a vital truth starts to emerge: Whatever consciousness dictates, the vehicle carries it out. Awakening isn't bound by the brain's training, which enforces linear, logical, cause-and-effect explanations, which have no bearing on what it means to escape the illusion. The escape is organized, timed, and dictated by your connection to pure consciousness.

Finding Your Wisdom

SELF-SUFFICIENCY

PURE CONSCIOUSNESS DOESN'T NEED ANYTHING OUTSIDE itself—it enjoys complete self-sufficiency. Looking around and seeing only consciousness in all directions, the source can say, "I am enough." This conjures up a visual image, if you like, of a field of light that extends in all directions as far as you can see. There is no horizon. If you start to travel across the field, the journey never leaves and never arrives anywhere but within the field. The source has nowhere to be, because it is always here and now.

This is the key that enables you to be self-sufficient, lacking nothing. In the waking dream, self-sufficiency is impossible, because fear, insecurity, and a sense of lack are always present, no matter how good your life becomes. A dream is pretending to be real, and when we buy into Maya, we can pretend to be secure and self-reliant, untouched by deep fears, particularly the fear of death. Hundreds of books have been written about the peril of the human condition, but a very simple fact is inescapable: The only security that is achieved inside the waking dream is a pretend security.

Maya's laws and rules can't help but be pretend. They are dream rules to hold a dream universe together. The whole complicated business of creating a physical universe over 13.8 billion years ago is a disguise. Behind the disguise, you and the source are one. You can say, "I am enough" once you see through the mask of matter that the physical world presents. Even if you are at the stage of merely contemplating what it might mean to wake up, you can start to live as if you were complete, whole, without fear, and lacking nothing.

That alone is non-pretend. Anytime you feel distracted by any situation that makes you feel unsafe, insecure, doubtful, or anxious, pause and remind yourself, "I am not touched by this, not in my essence. My true nature is beyond any situation."

This reminder might make you feel immediately calmer, less distracted, and more centered. It is also possible, however, that the situation will continue to dominate your attention. Either outcome is valid and acceptable. Your aim isn't to change the world around you by having higher, nobler, more spiritual thoughts. Your aim is to stop playing Maya's game according to Maya's rules. The reminder is useful in bringing you back to your purpose.

No matter how overwhelming life gets, self-sufficiency is your natural state. "You" in this case means your essence, the self that is emerging right this minute from the field of pure consciousness as it has since the moment you were born. Saying "I am enough" is just a thought like any other thought;

therefore, it is transient and easily escapes into the void where all thoughts vanish. The brain isn't self-sufficient, and nothing your brain can devise will do the trick. The brain is the wrong tool for the job when the job is waking up. Only awareness is the right tool for the job, and the more often you realize this fact, even for a moment, the closer you are to your source.

When the waking dream dissolves, So does the separate self

•

O F THE MANY WAYS THAT THE WAKING DREAM CONVINCES US that it is real, none is more powerful than fear. We've covered many urgent reasons to break free, but there is the element of fear to contend with. Everyone has lived with "I," the identity that is part of the waking dream. When you move in the direction of waking up, on the very threshold of becoming who you really are, "I" begins to panic, warning you that you are about to lose your identity. The separate self is the part of you that fears what will happen if you reject Maya once and for all.

There is good reason for panic—"I" isn't afraid for nothing. The sense of having a separate ego residing inside your body like a ghost in the machine doesn't survive awakening. Its existence is tied up in Maya because there is nowhere "I" can look where Maya is absent. The illusion being projected is everywhere. Like the ultimate in virtual reality devices, Maya's projection runs in, around, and through every experience. "I" justifies its existence by learning all the ins and outs that everyday life presents. No matter how skillfully you have navigated through life so far, your separate self can't follow you to your real self; it can't be blamed for fearing that all will be lost.

"I" gains its tremendous power by telling you that exiting the waking dream is tantamount to suicide. Fear has an advantage in any argument, namely, its emotional hold over you—fear doesn't have to prove that its warnings are factually true. Once you realize that you are being manipulated, you begin to stop listening to the voice of fear.

The advantage that places you above and beyond your fears is your ability to experience awakening. Every fearful expectation running through your mind is divorced from what really happens.

You aren't condemning your separate self to extinction. "I" will be reconfigured; it won't die. Think of a magician revealing how he pulls a rabbit out of a hat. Once you know the secret, the illusion is dead. The trick can still be performed to dazzle an audience that isn't in on the secret, but you won't be among them. Similarly, the whole physical setup of mind, body, brain, and universe will unfold to dazzle the unwary, but it will no longer dazzle you. By not participating in Maya's game, you drop the role of being a player, and since the only purpose that "I" has is to play along with the waking dream, your identity can never be the same once you are in on the trick.

Being awake is not the absence of self—it is the presence of your true self, beyond all boundaries and limitations.

This is where awareness takes over from all the mental activity that keeps churning out thoughts, feelings, sensations, hopes, fears, desires, and memories. That's the baggage that "I" carries around to feel real and alive. Subtract "I" from the equation, and the baggage goes with it. No wonder that awakening—the greatest single step you can take, a kind of spiritual rebirth—feels fatal at the level of fear. So how do you get around this fatal premonition?

The answer lies in the word *presence.* The backdrop of all experience is ever-present consciousness, like an eternal movie screen. The difference is that we can't turn off the movie, raise the lights, and see the screen. Instead, we must sense its presence. The mind has no practice doing this. Mental activity preoccupies every waking moment. If your mind suddenly had no content to grab your attention, the presence of consciousness would be obvious.

A brief glimpse of presence might not make an impression; it certainly wouldn't transform you on the spot. The silent gap in between thoughts brings such glimpses anytime you pause to notice it. Silent gaps don't even feel like experiences, more like nothing happening. But if you dive into the silence, it expands, and then its huge significance dawns. Silence is the womb of creation.

The journey of awakening consists of new ways to relate to presence. First it is unnoticed or glimpsed in a transient moment. Pay more attention, and presence stops being temporary. You sense it as our intimate companion. The next stage brings out the creativity that emerges from presence. You become involved in how life renews itself, like water pouring from a wellspring. Finally, when you have experienced presence deeply enough, you and it are one. Every vaunted attainment in spirituality, including the highest states of enlightenment, can be traced to the same journey taking place by paying attention to presence.

Finding Your Wisdom

PRESENCE

PRESENCE HAS ALWAYS HAD A SPECIAL SPIRITUAL MEANing. God is known by sensing a divine presence. In Eastern traditions, the equivalent is the presence of bliss, which is divine because it brings ecstasy. Presence is much more fundamental than any feeling, however. It is our connection to pure consciousness; therefore, it immerses us in the very womb of creation.

When you experience presence, personal awareness turns into something else. Here we enter the province of mystics. They convey what it is like to merge with the source, God, the field of pure consciousness—the terms being used are interchangeable. Consider a famous passage from the Spanish mystic St. John of the Cross: "I entered where there is no knowing, and unknowing I remained—transcending all knowledge."

What St. John testifies to is beyond everyday existence, therefore transcendent, yet there is nowhere to go to find the divine presence. It is more accurate to say that presence finds you. In a moment of total clarity, you realize that you are aware because awareness is the bedrock of existence. Your personal awareness is like a wave in the ocean. Whether the wave is big or small, whether it rises or falls, under all circumstances the wave and the ocean are one.

Presence, then, is your reminder of oneness; to use St. John's words, there is no "knowing or unknowing," because the experience is pure awareness without the content of thoughts. The words of mystics are playing catch-up. Their experience is demanding to be put into words even though it needed no words while it was happening. (Or as St. John puts it poetically, "I learned enormous things, but what I felt I cannot say . . . It was the perfect realm of holiness and peace.")

It is hard to talk about presence without becoming lofty and spiritual, which soon becomes misleading. Presence, including divine presence, is invisibly woven into everything. There isn't an issue about being humble or grand, not even an issue about God or not God. The simplest analogy is to ordinary things like the heat of the sun, the wetness of water, and the blue of the sky. They aren't things that involve intellectual understanding. Experiencing them tells its own story.

Pause for a moment and imagine that you have encountered a friendly extraterrestrial who also speaks English. "I'm struggling with some words," he says, asking for your help. "Can you write down a brief description of what wet, hot, and blue mean?" Of course, you won't be able to. Water is wet, and that's the whole story, just as the sun is hot and the sky is blue.

We all live in the presence of water, the sun, and the sky. Once you put it that way, presence isn't so mysterious. You realize how basic it is in every experience of the world, yet the physical building blocks of the world, the physics and chemistry that lie behind H_2O, stellar combustion, and the diffraction of sunlight, don't really touch the presence of life.

Because you can sense presence, you are the conduit for consciousness as it creates everything and gives it a special presence. Wetness, heat, and the color blue are bits of presence pointing you toward the whole of presence, which is cosmic and universal.

Seeking doesn't end when you know the truth.
Seeking ends when you *are* the truth.

S PIRITUALITY PRESENTS RIDDLES THAT SEEM DESIGNED TO frustrate anyone searching for answers. Yet these riddles are necessary to break the spell induced by Maya.

If you seek God, the soul, enlightenment, or bliss, your mind can aid you only so far, because it is conditioned to reinforce the waking dream, not to see through it. Where can a seeker go without the mind as an ally? This is where a riddle enters, and the riddle says, "What you seek is already here." At first glance this declaration seems to make the whole project of seeking pointless. There's nowhere to go if the goal of seeking is already here.

The reason that this riddle is necessary isn't to frustrate you or to pose some version of a Zen koan, like "What is the sound of one hand clapping?" A koan is meant to defeat the rational mind, forcing you to search for another way to find an answer. "What you seek is already here" serves a different purpose, to prevent you from going anywhere outside yourself. The mystical Indian poet Kabir points out the futility of seeking for higher truth in the external world: "You don't grasp the fact that what is most alive of all is inside your own house; and you walk from one holy city to the next with a confused look!"

This is sometimes called the paradox of the thirsty fish, who is driven to find a drink of water when it is surrounded by water. The fact that spiritual truth isn't found by looking outside yourself is the same as saying that no knowledge "out there" is of any use. The truth in spiritual terms has no connection to any other kind of search. All other searches, such as mapping the human genome or finding the cure for cancer, proceed by acquiring facts, data, measurements, and logical conclusions. Take away all that apparatus, and you are left with a startling realization: Spiritual seeking doesn't end when you know the truth. Seeking ends when you *are* the truth.

In other words, what you seek—God, the soul, enlightenment, life after death, and all other spiritual goals—is in your very being. Nothing is more intimate than being here. No experience replaces this fact or overrides it. (This explains why the riddle said, "What you seek is already here.") Yet the element of frustration doesn't automatically resolve itself, because when you turn your attention "in here," what you find is a storehouse of dream-stuff—all the beliefs, habits, memories, and old conditioning that mirror Maya. If the world "out there" holds no answers for the seeker, the world "in here" doesn't, either, not if Maya's rules govern the whole project of seeking.

The issue is only resolved by seeing very clearly that an object in the physical world, like a tree, a table, or a teacup, is paralleled by mental objects like thoughts, dreams, and wishes. Both kinds of objects are separate from you. It doesn't really matter, for example, if you see the Empire State Building, Leonardo Da Vinci's *Last Supper,* or a vision of the archangel Michael in the outside world or in your mind. There is still a gap between you and that object.

When this gap is closed, the observer and the object being observed become united. Then and only then can you become the truth you seek. Maya can't lead you to the state of unity, because the whole purpose of Maya is to create the illusion that separation is natural. Instead, it has taken the insights of poets, mystics, sages, and saints to point toward unity, as the great Sufi poet Hafiz does: "We have come into this exquisite world to experience ever more deeply our divine courage, freedom, and light."

As we established earlier, all seeking using the mind remains under the power of Maya—just another twist and turn in the collective dream. In the light of pure consciousness, you aren't the knower trying to know something special, a precious key that will fulfill you spiritually. In reality, you *are* the knowledge you seek, a living knowledge that spontaneously rises from the source. In the state of separation, reality always lies across a gap between "I" and the outside world. Maya is set up to allow for human progress, and we have been spectacularly successful at achieving advances in modern medicine, engineering, physics, computers, and any field where the rational mind can bring knowledge to replace ignorance.

But the rules of Maya forbid closing the gap because in one stroke the state of separation would collapse. At the same time, our collective dream would vanish. We would clearly see the folly of putting our entire focus on external progress, keeping the destructive side of technology in a compartment we ignore at our peril. Yet there is no comfort in such tactics. On this side of the gap, "I" feels the fear engendered by nuclear and biochemical weapons. The most destructive outcomes in the modern world horrifically magnify the wars, conflict, violence, tribalism, and nationalism from the past.

People are separate because the human mind is divided against itself. We hide from the horrors that loom "out there" because we deny that we are hiding from ourselves. This self-division isn't normal, no matter how much we have adapted to it. Maintaining the illusion of normalcy is a key part of the waking dream; we are afraid to unleash our demons. It takes courage, as Hafiz reminds us, to stop fooling ourselves. Closing the gap is a correction that returns us to where we are designed to be, at the center of creation, here and now, as pure consciousness flows spontaneously from the source.

Finding Your Wisdom

UNITY CONSCIOUSNESS

IT BEARS REPEATING THAT AWAKENING ISN'T MYSTICAL. It's a return to awareness as life's guiding principle. Enlightenment doesn't deserve to be considered rare. Countless people are awake, not just the sages and saints who have gained public recognition, usually to reinforce an organized religion. Every religion has traditionally used saints to justify its version of God. In that respect, the modern secular world has an ironic advantage—skepticism has made the issue moot about who has the most and best saints.

This advantage fades, unfortunately, when the main thrust of religion—to be reconnected with the divine—is sacrificed. It is urgent to replace oneness with God, which few people hope to attain or even believe in, offering instead oneness within ourselves—unity consciousness. This requires neither faith nor belief. There is no obedience to dogma or priests. You only need to have the experience as proof that unity is normal.

A powerful kind of evidence is offered by falling in love. At its most intense, you and your beloved merge, or so it seems on the inside. You cannot wait to see and touch your beloved, because this feels so real that the outside world cannot compare. Everyday life is suddenly a phantom, a flat scene of shifting images that is meaningless because it lacks love. Falling in love is all-embracing, which is why it deserves to be held up as an example of unity consciousness.

So why don't we fully embrace this state? Because there's

the accepted belief that falling in love is a kind of aberration. From the outside, without the lens of love, no one appears as a divine, perfect being worthy of worship. Lovers talk nonsense when they speak in such ecstatic terms. Time will bring a return to harsh reality, and as the spell of romance begins to lift, you and your beloved resume your status as separate egos, each with your own agenda. The sublime beauty of being in love gives way to the hard work of establishing a relationship, complete with the negotiations and frustrations that are part of everyday life.

Unless, of course, this entire perspective is wrong. Falling out of love, or doing without love altogether, is only normal by the rules that maintain the state of separation. The reason lovers return to their isolated egos is that "I" has been so thoroughly trained in living separately, looking out for number one, and placing self-interest above anyone else's interests. A solid, loving relationship resolves many issues raised by the selfish ego, but that's not the same as escaping from the state of separation.

Falling in love is a major escape, but you have experienced unity in smaller ways that need to be recognized and valued. The ego loses its grip whenever you are selfless and altruistic. Someone else's need becomes your own, just as empathy allows someone else's feelings to be your own. What is happening is a loss of boundaries, which is the key to unity consciousness. Unbounded wonder, the joy of creativity, ecstasy inspired by music and art: These are all unbounded experiences. The seed of unity consciousness has already been sown in everyone's life—it only requires the light of awakening to grow.

Deeply meaningful events like falling in love bring you into the light of truth. Staying in the light is impossible, however, when the ego claims ownership of the experience. To be selfless, in the sense of abandoning the ego and its self-centered agenda, is part of the maturing phase spiritually. What it takes is the intent to be reconnected with your source once and for all.

Here's a useful exercise for loosening the hold that the ego constantly exerts. As a means of experiencing non-separation, set aside a time simply to observe someone or something without expectations. Be with the act of seeing, listening, or feeling. You might watch a bird in flight and hear the sound of the wind or sit with someone and simply tune in to their presence. Notice how this shifts your attention away from all concerns of "I," "me," and "mine."

Empathy is even more striking in dissolving boundaries. Choose a person you interact with regularly. As you do, sense their feelings and inner state, rather than your own. Let a sense of empathy flow through you without trying to hold on to or analyze the experience.

These practices, done consistently and with intention, awaken a profound sense of unity, dissolving the illusion of separation to reveal your inseparable connection to hidden dimensions. You gain a clue that boundless awareness has always been your true nature.

The war between good and evil
Has a creative solution

T HE WAR BETWEEN GOOD AND EVIL IS ONE OF THE OLDEST AND most enduring narratives in human history. From ancient myths to modern headlines, we see this conflict playing out on every stage. But what if good versus evil isn't an inherent truth of existence, but rather a deeply ingrained belief, a lens through which we interpret the world? While atrocities such as genocide, murder, and abusive cruelty are undeniable, they are not proof of an absolute, external evil force. Instead, they reflect the complex interplay of human consciousness, shaped by separation and karma.

The root concept of good and evil has become so entrenched in our collective story that it feels inexorable, but awakening reveals the central role played by the human mind, not an unchangeable law of existence. As the Buddha observed, "It is a man's own mind, not his enemy or foe, that lures him to evil ways." This insight challenges us to look beyond simplistic labels of good and evil to examine the inner conflicts that give rise to suffering.

There is no way to determine when human beings first invented the war between good and evil. As with many things concerning the evolution of consciousness, there is no origin story, but one thing is certain. The concept was so powerful that it went viral, infecting every culture and era.

At some point—a time that once again we cannot pinpoint— amnesia set in. We collectively forgot that the source of good versus evil is ourselves. Inner conflict is at fault, and all inner conflict represents the mind divided against itself. In the state of separation, duality rules. As the Tao Te Ching declares, "When people see some things as beautiful, other things become ugly. When people see some things as good, other things become bad." In other words, every choice is classified as either/or. Good versus evil stands as an overwhelming example of how either/or can spin out of control and begin to lead a life of its own. However, in the wider context, the state of separation made the conflict inevitable.

Strange as it sounds, the fact that our remote ancestors invented both good and evil took enormous creativity. In the Book of Genesis, knowledge of good and evil happened all at once, in a decisive act when the serpent tempted Adam and Eve. In that one act, guilt and shame were born, paradise on Earth was lost forever, all innocence was destroyed, and humankind fell from grace. So many ideas are packed into a single sin that one can see how the concept of good versus evil had spread, in a viral way, one or two thousand years before the Christian era among the people of the Hebrew Bible.

Although the myth of the Garden of Eden is presented as the catastrophic beginning of human sin and misery, it can be read as a report on the lives that were being led at the time the story was told (the oral tradition traces Genesis back 1,000 to 2,000 years before it was written down around the fifth century BCE). As a report about living in the state of separation, an ancient myth is actually a true account, echoed in every culture that told tales of a lost paradise or a golden age. A disconnect from the source was being experienced, and myths were an attempt to explain how and why this happened.

It doesn't matter that we have no specific date for the advent of good and evil because the same waking dream is experienced here and now. Maya weaves good and evil into the mindset at any time for people who accept the waking dream as reality. It is impossible to extricate the duality of good and evil from the other dualities it is mixed up with—light and dark, creation and destruction, life and death, and so on.

Once you realize that duality itself is mind-made, the cosmic resonance of good versus evil is silenced. No supernatural forces are struggling in combat. The struggle exists in human awareness alone. Recognizing the mind-made nature of duality does not absolve us from moral responsibility. Unity consciousness is not an escape from reality but an invitation to see beyond the horrors woven into the waking dream. A single phenomenon—our disconnection from the source—explains everything without the need for the drama surrounding God and the gods versus Satan and other avatars of evil.

An inspiring quote from Rumi is also one of the first I ever read: "Out beyond ideas of wrong-doing and right-doing, there is a field. I'll meet you there." This is an invitation to achieve unity consciousness, which lies beyond all dualities, even those we most fear. When you stop being attached to your personal viewpoint, the end of separation is at hand, and with it, a realization that is mind-blowing. The medieval German mystic Meister Eckhart had the experience personally. He wrote, "The eye with which I see God is the same eye with which God sees me; my eye and God's eye are one eye, one seeing, one knowing, one love."

Take a few moments to reflect on your own thoughts and reactions throughout the day, and you'll begin to see that the potential for harm and goodness coexist in you. Fighting to keep badness in check is worthwhile, of course, but the pairing of good and evil must be transcended to find a permanent solution.

Finding Your Wisdom

NO ABSOLUTE EVIL

EVIL HAS NO SPECIAL PLACE IN CREATION. NO MALEVO-lent force looks down on humanity, determined to do us harm or to inspire evil actions in us. In the modern world, the notion of an evil being like Satan has waned, but that still leaves the question of where human evil comes from. It doesn't seem satisfying simply to call evil a concept. As we all know, monstrous acts of wrongdoing exist and always have. The spectacle of genocide reinforces the belief that human nature must be inherently evil or, at the very least, good and evil war within us, and the role of civilization is to tamp down inner evil. Otherwise, primitive violence will erupt from somewhere—a popular candidate in neuroscience is the lower or reptilian brain.

Yet none of this evidence proves that there is absolute evil anywhere, either inside or outside us. Even though the Judeo-Christian tradition espouses the existence of Satan as our ultimate adversary, St. Augustine, for one, cautions against such a belief: "Never fight evil as if it were something that arose totally outside of yourself." Wrongdoing exists on a spectrum, like all human behavior.

This perspective does not diminish the reality of suffering or the necessity to confront wrongdoing. The underlying vision comes from awakening instead. When we call a horrendous act "pure evil," the phrase is incorrect. Pure evil would be absolute, totally beyond the influence of pure good. If you take both misconceptions away, the most horrifying evil is human behavior taken to an extreme. That doesn't condemn human nature; it only illustrates how complicated we are. Evil has many causes tangled together. The reason evil hasn't been wiped out is that no one could possibly unravel all these causes, which exist not in evildoers exclusively but in everyone.

Accepting this truth leads to compassion and understanding, beginning with oneself. The shadows of so-called evil reside in your everyday behavior. Pause for a moment to examine if that's true. Are you capable of losing your temper or acting rashly? Are you in perfect control of all your impulses, including those you aren't proud of? Have you experienced intense shame and guilt that remains with you even today? Answering those few questions honestly begins to reveal how evil isn't a malevolent monolith but the distorted outgrowth of psychological traits present in everyone. Under bad circumstances, some factors permeate people's lives more than others: abuse, humiliation, low self-esteem, poverty, peer pressure, a family history of violence, mental illness. These elements constitute the toxic brew from which the worst evildoing arises, but if you trace them back from the extremes of evil, everything I've listed exists, at least in seed form, in everyone.

Understanding helps to clarify why human behavior can veer into horrible extremes, but only the intention to wake up takes you out of duality, at which point you stop participating in the drama of good versus evil.

Your true nature is always present. You do not have to seek it.

•

WE THINK OF SEEKERS GOING ON A PERSONAL PILGRIMAGE TO find God. Even outside a religious quest, *seeking* implies a goal. The spiritual path—meaning any spiritual path—is meant to take you to your goal. This seems reasonable enough. In an age of faith, an entire lifetime can be dedicated to seeking God, redemption, Heaven, forgiveness, or divine blessing. Were these goals ever reached? To be frank, no. Seeking becomes a perpetual activity that winds up in frustration. This is as true today as it was in the past.

In an age of faith, the fault lies with the seeker. The number of possible faults is open-ended. In the West, a seeker could be so sinful that redemption is denied. In Eastern traditions, where sin isn't blamed, the fault might be a lack of discipline in practicing meditation or preoccupation with the external world. The irony is that none of these reasons apply once you face the hard truth that seeking, even by the most pious, devoted, disciplined, and well-intentioned seekers, is a failure even before you begin.

What dooms seeking is a kind of paradox, and until you solve the paradox, true seeking cannot begin. True seeking isn't of the mind. It is the mind that dreams up goals in everyday life. Anything the mind sets out to achieve has a chance of succeeding. All it takes is connecting two points: Point A, where the goal is named (going to the gym, getting a better job, buying a house, or colonizing Mars), and Point B, where the project ends successfully.

Some projects don't succeed, as we all know, because something defeats us between Points A and B. It is only natural for spiritual seeking to be viewed the same way. The seeker starts out at Point A with a firm idea that God is waiting at Point B. If the project fails, something went wrong along the way.

But spiritual seeking is unique. There is no Point B; therefore, nothing awaits—not God, the eternal soul, redemption, Heaven, or enlightenment. This is where the paradox comes in. The mind is fooling itself when it imagines that the goal can be visualized, put into words, or reduced to a sequence of steps that brings spiritual growth. To put the paradox in a more positive light, seeking fails because what you seek is already here. No matter how exalted the goal, it is available in your true nature.

Which is how the paradox is resolved. Instead of pursuing a distant goal, which cannot be reached, returning to your true nature is always possible, no matter where in life you begin. You have a gift that transcends thinking, and therefore the thinking mind cannot interfere with it. The gift is self-awareness. Although everything else about mental activity is changing constantly, self-awareness—the sense of "I am"—is beyond change.

Self-awareness is the only absolute trait you possess, and you possess it in common with every other human being, and not just them. Every sentient being participates in consciousness, and it is possible, particularly among intelligent mammals like whales, dolphins, and primates, that some form of "I am" makes them aware that they, too, exist. We cannot deny other creatures their version of consciousness, and it isn't necessary to possess a mind filled with thoughts to be aware—just the opposite. The purest kind of "I am" might belong to the animal kingdom, free as it is from human thought.

Self-awareness in us cannot be created or destroyed. Since awakening is the state of being fully aware, the self-awareness you experience right now is enough. You need to make seeking a different sort of project, which takes place entirely by paying attention. Nothing more and nothing less enabled the most revered saints, sages, and enlightened masters to reach higher consciousness. The all-important factor is what you pay attention to.

In everyday life, people pay attention to experiences that affect their separate self, the "I" that has its agenda for getting ahead and being happy. Self-awareness isn't part of this agenda. Before you can say "I am happy," "I am lonely," or "I am excited," there is always and only "I am." The rest is filling in the blanks. As far as your ego is concerned, "I am X" is the whole point of being alive. X is the next thing you want or don't want, love or hate, want to run after or run away from.

It entirely escapes our notice that X isn't the important part of the sentence or thought. X is fickle, transient, unpredictable, and tied to pleasure and pain. These aren't criticisms. There is nothing you can desire, fear, want, wish for, fantasize about, or put into words that makes any difference to "I am." Distracted by a million and one things that pop up in our waking dream, it is no wonder that we have almost no acquaintance with "I am."

Turning the tables is the opening that awakening needs. You start paying attention to self-awareness. We can say, for the sake of convenience, that awareness can expand, evolve, aspire to high consciousness, and finally reach unity, but those are all thoughts, and thinking isn't the way to wake up. I know that "paying attention to self-awareness" sounds abstract and far removed from everyday life, but all of us already know how to pay attention.

The instant you started paying attention, which began soon after you were born, we can say you started exercising a gift. You might remember moments when your mind wandered and a teacher or parent admonished you: "Pay attention. You need to listen to this." They weren't talking about your ears or the auditory cortex where sound is processed. Paying attention is focused awareness. Not paying attention is unfocused awareness.

In this brief depiction, the entire spiritual path is laid out, and it doesn't matter if *spiritual* is included. Take anything you dearly love to do, and you have focused your attention on it willingly, eagerly, and without strain or effort. Awakening is no different, all the way to the most enlightened figure you revere. An entire pantheon of spiritual heroes and heroines will be occupied by everyday people who discovered—often to their amazement or consternation—that focusing on consciousness fits the same pattern as doing what you love right now. The spiritual path is something you want to join willingly, eagerly, and without strain or effort.

In a word, the spiritual path succeeds if you love it. The Spanish saint, Teresa of Avila, spoke from personal experience about the total absorption love brings: "It is love alone that gives worth to all things. The soul and God are alone in this state of union, and the soul only knows that it is happy, and this happiness is beyond its understanding."

Those words also describe the state of your true nature. Returning to your true nature can't be an abstract goal—it must be an act of love. Knowing that, a tremendous sense of relief sets in, because struggle, discipline, diligence, sacrifice, and single-minded dedication no longer matter (not that many people love them to begin with). All that matters is to say, "I see. I get it now." After that moment, the very thing you seek starts to seek you, as your true nature has been doing all the time.

Finding Your Wisdom

LOVING PRESENCE

I F YOU LOVE ANYTHING AT ALL, YOU CAN LOVE THE spiritual path. The only requirement is to know that you are connecting with your true nature. That's a unique kind of love, because it lies at the root of everything else you love, whether it is dark chocolate, your family, or the music of Bach. In all those cases, you are tapping into your true nature, but at a distance from the source. You are loving something that is part of the waking dream. In fact, anything you can name by saying "I love X" remains inside the boundaries of Maya, because naming is a mental activity.

Your true nature is built into your awareness, which makes it ever-present and indestructible. Here is where unconditional love lies. It isn't something you seek, as when you want unconditional love from someone else or aspire to offer it to someone else. Unconditional love is essential to your being. Therefore, it has its own presence, its own allure. You are attracted to it simply by wanting to know who you are.

Since every step that gets you closer to your true nature is guided by love, it takes no effort, thought, or diligence to follow a path you love. To give a homey analogy, if you smell the warm scent of bread baking, it's a pleasure to follow that aroma just as much as the pleasure of eating the bread. Instead of using your nose, however, on the path to your true nature, you follow your self-awareness.

Another analogy from everyday life will clarify how this works. In your mind's eye, see the face of someone you love. Notice that you are also summoning the warm feeling of affection in your heart. Put your attention there, allowing the image of the face to fade. What you are feeling is the presence of love. It exists without that person being in the room or even alive. You don't leaf through a catalog of memories. The awareness of love hangs in the air, so to speak. (In Sanskrit this space has a specific name, *Chit Akash*, where *Akash* means "space" and *Chit* is "awareness.")

Your true nature is connecting with you in awareness anytime you sense its presence. Love is a cherished aspect of your true nature, but that nature also encompasses intelligence, creativity, empathy, wisdom, and every other higher human value. Love is perhaps the easiest to connect with because we are used to its presence, starting as infants loving our parents. Again, to put this into words shouldn't be mistaken for the experience.

To align yourself with the path, noticing the presence of love is valuable because it carries you effortlessly to a subtler area of awareness. There is never anything you need to do in your awareness except to pay attention. There are time-honored techniques that are like training exercises for paying attention, such as meditation, yoga, contemplation, inner reflection, and mindfulness.

At some point on the path, you are likely to become interested in one or more of these practices, but they shouldn't cloud the true nature of paying attention, which is effortless. Loving attention is effortless and pleasant, which makes it much less likely that you will fall into the non-compliance that causes many people to take up meditation or mindfulness, only to drop it over time.

You can turn loving presence into a gentle kind of practice simply by noticing it. Anytime you find yourself in a loving state, let your attention go to the feeling. Deep love, romantic love, and profound love are rare experiences in everyday life. But noticing something you simply enjoy allows you to focus your attention on the essence of the experience, which is loving presence. You don't have to name it. Being with it is all you need.

Once you find it easy and natural to connect with this aspect of your true nature, you won't need the aid of a stimulus that triggers loving presence. You can summon it in your awareness on its own. Loving presence exists very close to "I am." It isn't pure consciousness, but a subtle expression of pure consciousness emerging into the world.

At any moment when you feel calm and content, not from any triggering event but simply from the place where you find yourself, notice the presence of your own being. If there is a feeling of lightness, warmth, or bliss, all the better. But the essential thing is to commune with the presence of your true nature. It is the beginning and end of the path, and every step along the way.

Wisdom cannot be taught or learned, Yet nothing is more valuable

•

WISDOM ARRIVES WHEN YOU ARE COMPLETELY CLEAR ABOUT yourself and the world. Your awareness is here and now, effortlessly witnessing any situation, whether of joy or suffering, with perfect equanimity. An image from Indian spiritual traditions compares an enlightened person to "a lamp at the door," sitting at the threshold between the relative world and the transcendent. This image comes alive every year during Diwali, the festival of lights, where lamps (*diyas*) are placed at the entrances of homes. This signifies the light of inner wisdom radiating outward to dispel external darkness.

Your potential to radiate spiritual light is always available. If you could see yourself with total clarity, you would realize that you have always been poised between the physical world and what lies beyond. Awakening frees you to live in the light and only there. Such total clarity, by itself with nothing more added, is wisdom.

As beautiful as this sounds, there is still a clash between the waking dream and reality. By facing in both directions, the desire to live in the light can't erase what people call real life. Rumi puts the clash poetically: "Wisdom tells us we are not worthy; love tells us we are. My life flows between the two." That might sound like a contradiction with the peace that passes understanding, Jesus's teaching about being established with God or, in non-religious terms, being established in your real self, permanently connected to your source. In truth, wisdom leads someone to voluntarily live in both realms simultaneously. The transcendent isn't really beyond the here and now once you see that light permeates everything.

Many things are the reverse of what they seem to be in the waking dream, and nothing is more distorted than our view of wisdom. The typical image of wisdom conjures up a venerable graybeard sitting in solitude inside a cave. This Eastern image has crowded out the popular Western image of a kindly grandfather. Age is common to both stereotypes. Whether grandfather or guru, the old wise man gathers the young around him to impart his wisdom.

These benign images don't look distorted, but they support a completely misguided idea, that wisdom is something you learn through experience and can pass on to someone else. Certainly, there's a valid role to be filled, known as mentoring. An experienced teacher imparts the fruit of his experience. Not only is this not the same as wisdom, but a seminal figure in Greek philosophy, Socrates, took poison over this very issue. He opposed a class of teachers in Athens known as the Sophists, whose profession was to impart wisdom to the privileged youth of the city. (*Sophist* is derived from the Greek word for wisdom, *sophia*.)

Socrates was accused and convicted of corrupting the youth of Athens when he denied that wisdom, or any version of higher truth, could be taught, which therefore meant it couldn't be learned, either. He was sentenced to death. The story of Socrates drinking poisonous hemlock symbolizes someone willing to die for the truth, but at heart, the point was that the Sophists were guilty of teaching untruth. Or, as we would put it, they were teaching their high-born pupils how to remain trapped in the waking dream while believing that they were attaining true wisdom.

The situation hasn't drastically changed. A reputation for being spiritually advanced can be gained by laying out wise advice, uttering profound thoughts, and teaching from a loftier plane. All the books, talks, lessons, retreats, and devoted followers of enlightened masters can't help but remain under the sway of Maya. The whole spiritual setup has no ultimate validity because it is mind-made. But, as we saw, playing by Maya's rules also reveals some loopholes, cracks in the dream that point to an escape route.

The loophole here, as you might already have guessed, is the lamp at the door. The light of wisdom shines through even in a dream. In India, the most revered figure who taught about unity consciousness was Adi Shankara, the preeminent Indian seer, who taught this: "Like the sun, wisdom lights up the whole world. It shines above and below, in all directions." True wisdom, if you can find it in inspirational books and teachings, exists in words only if the words make you feel more awake, and this happens only if they contain the light that shines everywhere.

Finding Your Wisdom

SEEING THE LIGHT

DUALITY OPERATES THROUGH OPPOSITES, AND IF YOU live in separation, light and dark are eternal opposites. We use them everywhere you look. Being in the light is like being in the right. Being in the dark makes you benighted. Light has a host of positive connotations; dark has a contrasting host of negative connotations. But like all mind-made opposites, this one falsifies reality. Spiritually, light has no opposite, because when you strip away all the connotations, light is pure awareness. It is absolute, eternal, unborn, and unchanging.

Once again, we are faced with something ungraspable. Light is easy to grasp when you have darkness to contrast it with. Everything is relative, and we live with our own personal light and shadow, good and bad, right and wrong. Nothing in the relative world can be absolute. It is inspiring to read that there is light that permeates everything, everywhere, all the time. But absolute, eternal light is alien to the everyday world, where no such light is evident.

Awakening allows you to see the light. It's the same as the definition of wisdom—seeing yourself and the world with total clarity. Clarity is an experience you can identify with. There is a real phenomenon of being able to visually see (or mentally process) a subtle light that illuminates things: Seeing auras is a genuine experience for those who have a subtle sense of sight. Leaving such a specialized ability aside, achieving clarity is universal; it is open to everyone.

If you wonder about seeing the light as an experience that applies to you, a blinding revelation isn't necessary. Clarity visits you in many guises; for example, when you feel that life is vibrant, when you experience how Nature is endlessly renewed and fresh, when your body feels physically light, or when your mood lightens despite all the cares in the world. Everyone has had at least occasional glimpses of such experiences.

A deeper experience is the light of awareness, which is clarity itself instead of the by-products just listed. Anything that fits the description of revelation—epiphany, inner vision, intuition, or insight—arrives by the light of awareness; you don't use your thinking mind to have such experiences. They are our default. Sunlight or the light from the stars is invisible until awareness transforms it. In many ancient cultures, the five senses traveled out from a person's mind, the opposite of the modern view that the five senses process data coming in from the outside world.

Both views need awareness. The raw data delivered by electromagnetism sets up sight, touch, taste, and smell, while the physics of air vibrations sets up hearing. The data has no choice but to be raw. It takes an experience in human awareness to create what we call sights, sounds, textures, tastes, and smells. If you adopt the model of the ancient world, awareness travels out into the world to contact the same raw data, bringing its transformative power with it.

Either explanation will serve. In the end, no explanation is needed. Maya merges human awareness with the world, while leaving out an important—in fact, all-important—point. There is no separate person seeing, hearing, touching, tasting, and smelling. There is only awareness in the act of knowing itself. The spiritual light that mystics perceive everywhere is just another way to express that pure consciousness is the source shared by all observers, all the things we observe, and the act of transformation that makes the five senses work. The whole world wouldn't work without pure consciousness.

In a word, every experience you have ever had took place in the light. You were designed to see the light as your default. This is what makes you the co-creator of reality as it flows in, around, and through you.

No one and nothing Is in charge of the universe

THE DREAMS WE HAVE IN OUR SLEEP ARE JUMBLED AND SUR-real, like disjointed action movies that rivet our attention without actually making sense. When you wake up, everything returns to making sense. Maya provides a setup that feels reliable. Time moves forward, action is followed by reaction, and cause and effect are in operation. This reliability is a major reason that hardly anyone realizes that they need to wake up a second time.

But when humankind began to ask the big questions—*Who created the world? Is God overseeing what happens? Is fate an invisible force behind the scenes?*—reliability collapsed. Looking to a higher power was supposed to explain how life works. Instead, God or the gods were fickle, as liable to punish as to reward, turning a blind eye to human suffering, and permitting the most terrifying natural disasters. It took centuries, but, eventually, the total unreliability of a higher power became an existential crisis in the modern world.

A God who allows genocide, totalitarianism, pandemics, and ecological disaster failed on two fronts. Help from a higher power was absent, and humankind wasn't saved from itself. It seemed irrefutable that no higher being was in charge. This left a vacuum that prompted nothing but dread. A world ruled by random chance, pitiless Nature, and the worst aspects of human behavior has become a frightening reality.

Another possibility arises, however. The fact that our waking dream has turned into a nightmare doesn't negate the fact that it is just a dream. Waking up is the answer to existential dread. The vacuum left by a departed God is imaginary. Pure consciousness hasn't been affected; it fills every vacuum with a flow of creative intelligence.

Intelligence is a hot-button issue if your worldview promotes randomness as the only source of events, including everything that has happened since the Big Bang. With no one in charge, the responsibility for holding chaos at bay goes to the natural laws that govern the universe. Even then, cosmology has veered into the multiverse theory, which makes our universe a winner among trillions of other universes where human DNA never appeared.

But what if natural laws like gravity and electromagnetism aren't in charge, either? As emotionally wrenching as it was to give up God or any other higher power, it is rationally wrenching to give up natural laws. When they become unreliable, so do time and space, which need natural laws as part of the cosmic scheme, and vice versa.

Yet the attempt to put *something* in charge is also doomed. The laws of physics and chemistry created the physical universe, but they emerged from nowhere and nothing. It defies the mind to locate the building blocks of time before time began or to locate a place outside space where space began. Reduce the universe to its most basic components, and suddenly the whole setup goes poof! All that's left, clinging by a thread, are imagined mathematical hyperspaces that will never be tangible.

Much complexity has been skipped over in this thumbnail description, but the essence of the problem is undeniable. The biggest questions lead to nothing, no one, and nowhere. Either the situation is tragic or, amazingly enough, amusing. Frightened by our mind-made nightmare, we've overlooked that dreams by their very nature come to an end. Waking up is always the only real experience anyone can ever have. Once you escape the state of separation, you can laugh at "no one, nothing, and nowhere," because, in reality, the field of consciousness is everything, everywhere, all at once.

Maya's setup often turns the truth on its head. That's what happens when we demand that someone or something should be in charge, lording it over us. If you are immersed in the flow of consciousness as creativity pours from the source, the concept of an overlord is pure fantasy. Being here now *just is.* That's not a curse. Contrary to the illusory setup of Maya, the setup of being here now is real. Every hope, promise, dream, and wish is fulfilled from it, including the resolution of everything in the future that holds terror in our waking dream but creative promise in the awakened life.

The greatest spiritual guides and teachers have repeated this truth, which was needed in times of fear, all the more because there has never been a time when fear didn't loom. A teaching of the Buddha is especially inspiring: "The whole secret of existence is to have no fear. Never fear what will become of you; depend on no one. Only the moment you reject all help are you freed."

Finding Your Wisdom

KARMA

WHEN LIFE IS A STRUGGLE, THERE IS ALWAYS SOMETHING the mind fights against, hoping "If only I can get past this, everything will be fine." Hope can ignite the way forward, but it would be much better to vanquish struggle at its root. It is part of our waking dream to believe that some hidden force is out there, its entire purpose being to thwart us.

This hidden force, known in the Indian tradition as karma, has no designs to harm or thwart us. In modern terms, karma is cause and effect, the simple interaction when A bounces off B, action leading to reaction. Saddling karma with spiritual meaning only deepens the illusion that someone or something is in charge. Karma doesn't rule your life; you aren't a puppet of fate, whatever name it goes by.

Far from being a hidden or higher power, karma can be broken down into rational components. First, karma is a vehicle for carrying the past into the present, just the way your genes do. Genes transfer physical traits, while karma is subtler. It carries forward the consequences of past actions. In popular lore, these actions, being good or bad, carry forward reward and punishment. You get what you deserve from a prior lifetime.

Such a claim can't be proved or disproved, which makes it useless for all intents and purposes. The only lifetime that can be experienced is here and now. There is room to allow that a person with the right subtle abilities can retrieve information that confirms reincarnation, but what good are old stories when all stories are part of the waking dream? So-called bad karma is the unintended consequence of past actions, but this is of no practical value, either, because unintended consequences arrive all the time from every direction. They can be good, bad, or indifferent. There's no reason to be anxious in advance. Once you've rationally dismantled karma, none of its components are mystical or supernatural.

In everyday life, the past overlaps the present in countless ways. We cope, adapt, and move on. But nothing overrides the reality that karma, like everything else in the setup of Maya, is ultimately taking place in a dream state. Only in the dream does it have any power to convince us. Shadows from the past are like any other shadow, vanishing instantly when exposed to the light.

The world appears different
In different states of consciousness

•

No TWO PEOPLE SEE THE WORLD IN THE SAME WAY, FOR MANY reasons, beginning with biology. Your biology shifts and changes in different states of consciousness. For example, if you're in a state of fear, your body responds with inflammation and heightened cortisol levels. Conversely, when you're in a state of love, your biology releases feel-good hormones like oxytocin and endorphins, creating a sense of bliss and well-being. As you change, the appearance of the world shifts—no one who has gone through a period of depression needs to be told that feeling sad and hopeless inside turns the world flat and unwelcoming.

Awakening reaches much deeper, however, creating a complete transformation in how the world appears. Biology is relevant here, too. When you're asleep at night, your biology is metabolically different from when you're awake. Dreams that come in REM sleep are marked by signature brain-wave patterns. To accept that you are perceiving the real world when you open your eyes in the morning is unreliable—you are only seeing what your state of consciousness permits.

Before awakening, everything is relative, meaning that how you relate to the world is always shaky, with no true permanence. When you're fearful, the world appears dangerous. When you're angry, the world appears hostile. When you're in love, everything seems beautiful. As a result, you have personalized the world, undercutting any possibility that two people can share the same reality. All kinds of mind-made filters interfere with clarity of vision, including your self-image and the story you have created about your life, along with your core beliefs, social pressures, and much more.

You have been navigating through life cocooned inside a personal reality that you attempt to defend and keep stable. The ego hates and fears instability. Everyone knows that they have bad habits, and people complain about the boredom of routine work. Yet habit and routine are the mainstays for keeping everything stable. "I am what I am; don't try to change me" is the ego's mantra.

The result for almost everyone is a contradiction. The appearance of the world is constantly shifting, yet pretending to be stable is a primary agenda. It's understandable why we don't break out of this contradiction. The ego doesn't want to lose control; your self-image needs protecting; your story makes you feel unique. Living inside a contradiction creates anxiety with so many overlapping agendas to defend. Yet none of them are worth defending once you see that you are trying to stabilize a waking dream.

Personal reality blocks "real" reality. Yet something inside us knows how futile the entire enterprise is. The hidden secret is that you don't have to relate to the world. You can allow your biology, perceptions, mental activity, moods, and all the rest of it to be whatever they happen to be. Your role isn't to dismantle the game of opposites that Maya has set up. Your role is to see through the illusion, transcending the relative world's instability for something permanent, safe, reliable, stable, and calm—the very things the ego is pretending to have found.

A new state of consciousness is the only escape route, and as with the states of consciousness you experience already—waking, sleeping, and dreaming—the appearance of the world changes in higher states of consciousness. Seeing through the illusion is a doorway. Beyond it lie experiences of expanded awareness, clarity, the end of suffering, and bliss. Religious traditions express this change in terms of a fallen world suddenly becoming divine. To quote Thomas Merton, "We are living in a world that is absolutely transparent, and God is shining through it all the time. This is not just a nice story or a fable, it is true."

Awakening should be portrayed as a transition into a new state of consciousness, not as the end of the journey. Studies of Tibetan Buddhist monks have verified changes in biology and brain activity that parallel a new state of consciousness. In terms of brain-wave patterns, nothing in the ordinary waking state comes close. With awakening, a new journey begins until you reach unity consciousness, when any hint of separation has vanished.

Finding Your Wisdom

BEFORE AND AFTER

WHEN WORDS DESCRIBE THE STATE OF AWAKENING, THE closest they can come is a near miss. I can write about the difference between being convinced by the waking dream and seeing with total clarity after awakening. The before-and-after picture is useful in making the awakened life look attractive. But "before and after" are worse than a near miss. Both words are trapped in our perception of time. It is nearly impossible not to look at a sequence like birth, aging, and death as proof of how time operates.

Yet awakening reveals that our participation in time is basically a long-standing habit, and as with many long-standing habits, we don't stop to examine this one. If we did, it would dawn on us that, like the world, time changes in different states of consciousness. Ingrained with conventional clock time, before and after are measured in linear intervals of seconds, minutes, days, and so on. In dreams, time is surreal and woozy. In dreamless sleep, consciousness blanks out, removing all perception, including time.

All this changes with awakening, which shifts your perception to now. Now isn't an interval of time. It is a focus of awareness. One instant of now is the same as every other, lifting you out of clock time. You can easily approximate what the eternal now feels like. Say a word, any word, such as *hippopotamus.* Pause a few seconds, then say the word again. Did it get older? No. Now stand up and walk around the room humming a tune, any tune, like the Beatles' "Let It Be." Are you carrying the melody to a new place as you walk? No again. States of consciousness, even our everyday waking state, don't obey ordinary habits of time and space.

Getting a little closer to reality, imagine that you are thinking, talking, humming music, or doing the dishes, all while not being tied to time or space. The only difference between this state of consciousness and the small exercise you just performed is that it is permanent. You are constantly here now. It bears repeating that this isn't mysticism. There was no "before" the Big Bang or "outside" the space that the stars and galaxies are hurtling through. The Big Bang produced the here and now that is the actual state of the universe and everything in it, including you and me.

In a very real way, another universe, if it happens to exist, is like a different state of consciousness. Pure consciousness, as the source of creation, wouldn't be affected, but the categories of time, space, matter, and energy would shift. Maybe in this different universe nothing changes except that human beings are all psychic or have a resting body temperature of 85°F, slowing life to a snail's pace. Their perception would shift to adapt to those conditions. One can even imagine a universe, for example, constructed entirely from dark matter and energy. The human brain cannot adapt to dark matter and energy in our universe, even though they exist in vastly overwhelming proportion to the visible universe. An unimaginable state of consciousness would need to exist.

Awakening, however, is far from unimaginable. In the short exercise just described, the habit of "before and after" was undermined in favor of "here now." Such glimpses bring awakening closer as a possibility. Realizing the possibility only takes a dedication to the one thing needed for awakening: paying attention.

Your internal dialogue Blocks pure knowing

EVERYDAY LIFE IS DRIVEN BY THINKING AND FEELING; THE awakened life is driven by pure knowing. That's a crucial difference that determines in many ways how your life turns out. In the state of separation, the mind is tangled up inside itself. There is constant chatter, which Buddhism calls "monkey mind." There is indecision, when you are torn between one impulse and its opposite. These are just two aspects of the running conversation you have with yourself all the time, known as your internal dialogue.

The internal dialogue was born of thought, and the voice you hear in your head is a kind of background thinking, much like an engine that keeps running on its own momentum even after it is switched off. Calling the internal dialogue a conversation masks how complex it really is. "I" isn't one entity in the state of separation but a host of fragmented voices. Imagine for a moment that you are a nervous bride the week before her wedding who is suddenly assailed by doubts. An interior struggle takes place between doubt and certainty. (Do I love him? Of course I do. Does he love me? He says he does. But does he love me enough? Maybe he's not the one. Etc.) Her internal dialogue struggles to reach an answer, yet there's no reliability in the voices she hears. They are fragments of the same "I" that creates all the confusion.

Pure knowing is the remedy for a mind that cannot trust itself. At the source there is no gap between question and answer. This is known in Buddhism as *pratītyasamutpāda*, which holds that every question and its answer arise together. This is a completely different experience from the thinking mind, which poses a question and then searches for an answer. To get a glimpse of the question and answer being seamlessly one without a gap, ask yourself a simple question: "Am I aware?" Notice that the answer is certain without having to think.

Pull back a little, and the issue of questions and answers points to a larger truth: Everything in consciousness is connected with everything else. A lofty term for this is *the interdependency of being,* but your body needs no concepts or words for a basic fact of survival, namely, every cell in the body relates to every other. The body as a whole survives on heart, brain, lungs, liver, and all other organs eavesdropping on each other. Cells that go rogue in one organ, as prostate or ovarian cancer does, destroy interdependence and eventually bring down the whole body.

Your internal dialogue contains aspects that have gone rogue. Stubborn, irrational beliefs, for example, are immune to reason. Anxiety ignores persuasion from other voices that say there is nothing to be anxious about. Caught in the middle, you don't know which voice to trust. Throw in the voices that express low self-esteem, self-judgment, criticism, pessimism, suspicion, and envy, and your internal dialogue, even when it seems pleasant, has the potential for disaster. At the very least, your mind becomes a befuddling hodgepodge of mental wandering without a center. When the internal dialogue turns distressing, therapists face a difficult challenge.

Despite all this, it's a mistake to look upon your mind as an enemy of your happiness, because awareness isn't the same as thinking and feeling; it transcends both. The solution in Eastern traditions is to quiet the chattering mind through mindfulness and meditation, but this prescription faces the same challenge. Everyone has developed thought patterns that feel permanent, so even the worst thoughts run on sheer momentum, repeating the past as protection against fear of change.

A better understanding revolves around the concept of captivating the mind, known in Sanskrit as *manoharmana*. In everyday language, the tendency of the mind is to be fascinated by whatever is beautiful, truthful, blissful, and creative. Those qualities emanate from the source. They catch your attention because, ultimately, you and the source are one. Pure knowing has the advantage that it is inherently captivating. The mind prefers truth, beauty, bliss, and creativity over their opposites. Pure knowing has a second advantage: It brings a sense of certainty. At this moment you know with total certainty that you are alive and aware, the prime example of pure knowing.

Awakening would be impossible without manoharmana. Everyone's internal dialogue is incessant. It won't stop by itself, and meditation, when it brings a deeper sense of quiet and calm, is only temporary; once you open your eyes, the active mind persists. It's important to understand that the natural tendency of your mind is to favor bliss, beauty, truth, and creativity. Knowing this, you can take a different stance to your internal dialogue. Favor the voices that represent the fascination of manoharmana. Pay as little attention as possible to negative voices.

When self-judgment tries to win your attention, think to yourself, "That has never gotten me anywhere. I don't need it anymore." When caught in a dilemma, be aware that the two voices arguing in your head are fragments of the same "I" that is confused. Say to yourself, "This arguing leads nowhere. All my experience confirms that both sides are unreliable." There are also practices from the therapeutic arsenal, like immediately replacing a negative thought with a positive one. If a voice in your head says, "You never win," pause and consider the times when you have won, even in small ways. Or think, "It's not about winning and losing."

Despite the constant mental chatter, you are not a monkey mind. You are an expression of pure consciousness. This is the primary motivation behind awakening, to know once and for all who you are.

Finding Your Wisdom

MENTAL MICROCHIPS

W<small>E'VE ALL ADAPTED TO OUR INTERNAL DIALOGUE,</small> which is inescapable in the state of separation. There is no resolution of the constant back-and-forth that is the default mode of a divided mind. Awakening solves the problem, but I don't want to give the impression that there is nothing you can do on the path to awakening. You can reframe any situation to bring clarity. Clarity and understanding counter confusion and conflict.

Seen clearly, repetitive negative thoughts are like microchips wired to send the same signal anytime they are triggered. These microchips got planted by bad experiences. For example, if you have failed at something important, an impression is left in your memory. In Sanskrit the word *vasana* applies—impressions from the past that continue to cling. Any strong experience, especially a negative one, creates a vasana, which delivers the same message (You are unlovable. You'll never win. This is hopeless. What's wrong with you? Etc.) anytime it is triggered. Microchips are hardwired without the possibility of change, no matter how much you resist, argue, persuade, or ignore. It is better to try to unplug them.

Vasanas are plugged in by emotion. They imprint your memory of fear, victimization, humiliation, defeat, disapproval, and abuse. The purpose is to warn you, but the actual result is rote repetition. Fear crops up in situations that aren't fearful. But like a scolding parent, the vasana claims that feeling afraid is for your own good, when what you want is the freedom to decide for yourself.

In practical terms, when a fearful, self-judging, or critical voice talks to you, don't pay attention to the message. Pay attention to how it feels. Getting past the feeling is how you unplug the microchip. Pause, feel whatever is there, and let awareness begin to dissolve the feeling. Take deep, steady breaths. You can also think, "I don't need this message. Thanks for the warning, but I have other options." Don't fight or resist, however. Let awareness do the unplugging.

If you are comfortable, stay with the feeling until it fades. Sometimes that's as simple as waiting for a moment or two. Really stubborn feelings need more time to dissolve, not by sitting through them until you are uncomfortable but by staying in your comfort zone. You will always have an opportunity to address the same message again. Hard, stubborn vasanas can be dissolved with awareness, even when the process goes forward in small steps.

The important thing is to realize that your internal dialogue is a symptom of the state of separation. There will be many opportunities to reset your mental default by paying attention to experiences that convey beauty, truth, bliss, and creativity. They are your true allies on the spiritual path.

Consciousness takes delight In witnessing itself

•

WHEN YOU LOOK AT SOMETHING THAT DELIGHTS YOU—
a gorgeous sunset, the face of someone you love—consciousness is
taking delight in seeing itself. Something beyond the individual "I"
is enjoying itself. As a person, you are the vehicle for this delight.
Therefore, your role in the cosmic design is vastly greater than you
imagine. Rumi puts it beautifully when he says, "Don't act small. You
are the universe in ecstatic motion."

The isolated separate "I" isn't suitable for such a role. It can't help
but act small, examining every situation throughout the day to decide
"Do I like this or not?" In other words, the ego is consumer shopping,
treating the world like a marketplace for experiences. There is a gap
between you and the experience you like or dislike. Call it the gap of
decision-making. In this gap you make your choice to accept or reject
whatever comes your way.

Without realizing it, you are interfering with your true nature.
It exists in the flow of consciousness, which is a continuous process. From within itself, consciousness creates and at the same time
watches creation with a sense of delight. Your ego doesn't imagine
that this is possible. What about all the negative experiences that
will inevitably crop up? You might be among the fortunate ones
who are never afflicted with poverty, abuse, natural disaster, or family crises. But the fear of what might happen afflicts the separate self,
disconnecting you from your true nature. As long as duality exists,

even the best life is overshadowed by the possibility of pain and suffering.

Awakening presents the solution, but it is a radical one. You abandon the viewpoint of "I" and replace it with the viewpoint of consciousness itself. Now duality no longer creates fear. You witness every situation without involvement. Delight comes from the love of creation, pure and simple, like an artist who takes delight in painting, no matter what the subject is. To quote Rumi again, "Love is from the infinite and will remain until eternity." Except for love, nothing you see will remain forever.

Without a doubt this is a radical shift. In the state of separation, it is inconceivable that the worst horrors and tragedies in history can be viewed with love. But that's not what happens. Witnessing brings awareness to the situation, and then whatever is needed in a bad situation is available. If "I" is distressed, horrified, or simply sad, those emotions can remain as they are. But the witness isn't affected, just as the light from a movie projector isn't affected by events on the screen. The role of the witness is to bring the light of awareness to any experience. The light is inseparable from love.

I realize that such a description seems grossly unfair. Where is compassion for those who suffer? The root of the word *compassion* is "to suffer with." Faced with other people's suffering, the separate self either suffers with them or turns away. The two choices are pain or indifference. That's why witnessing must be experienced, to find out for yourself that another viewpoint exists. Descriptions of the witness do it no justice. Only awakening proves that compassion can exist without pain.

In Sanskrit the witness is known as *sākṣī*, whose roots mean "the one who sees." Seeing turns out to be crucial. In every experience, "I" thinks that it, the separate person, is the one who sees. In reality, the one who sees—whether you are awakened or not—is the witness. The witness isn't a person. It is an aspect of consciousness. By its very nature consciousness knows, but it also sees. That is your true nature as well. Knowing and seeing are innate in you, without judgment or emotion.

There's a process in moving from the viewpoint of "I" to the viewpoint of the witness. The eternal delight and love that Rumi and other mystics glorify reaches its fullness in unity consciousness. But you can know yourself as the witness long before that.

You are witnessing in moments when your awareness comes to life. You might be looking at something that fascinates you. Unexpectedly, you might feel light or disembodied. Moments of utter peace and calmness cause "I" to fade away, leaving only the witness. You might have the uncanny experience that you aren't the one involved in a situation, as if it were happening to someone else while you look on. Awe and wonder also bring the witness into intimate contact with you.

The difference between these experiences and the awakened life is that in the latter the witness doesn't come and go. You realize first-hand what it means to be in the world but not of it. In religious terms, you have entered the state of grace. That's a lovely description, but saying that consciousness is taking delight in witnessing itself applies outside any religious context. Either way, your true nature is revealing itself. The witness is your essence, not an incidental choice or a decision you've decided to make. We saw before that the highest states of consciousness are achieved simply by paying attention. The one who pays attention is the witness and no other.

Finding Your Wisdom

DETACHMENT

ONE QUALITY OF AWAKENING HAS A BAD NAME, AND THAT is detachment. As a separate self, acting detached has almost no social value. It is positive to get involved instead of sitting on the sidelines. In that context, detachment is viewed as indifference. Against this background, detachment is even harder to accept as a spiritual trait. You have to look deeper, and then you see that spiritual detachment is far from indifference; it is a profound release, giving you freedom from attachment. Realizing how attached you have been—to ego, self-image, old conditioning, memory, and material rewards—you treasure the release that detachment brings. The Spanish mystic St. John of the Cross taught that in detachment the soul discovers true freedom and serenity. Freedom and serenity are qualities of awareness in themselves.

Spiritual detachment is better expressed as non-attachment. (In Sanskrit the word is *vairagya*.) Non-attachment has positive connotations. To convey that you are open-minded, it's common to say, "I'm not attached to my position." The same applies to a trial judge administering the law impartially, not being attached to one outcome over another. In other words, the experience of detachment doesn't have to carry a negative connotation. Still, finding a more palatable term doesn't really get at the spiritual value of detachment.

That value, as described in Vedanta, is "the ability to remain unaffected by the play of opposites." This isn't a possibility in the state of separation, where the setup of Maya is nothing but the play of opposites. Moments of detachment count for little against years of attachment when every desire is attached to being fulfilled. "I want X" isn't satisfied until X is attained. Can you have a desire and not care how it turns out? For the ego, no. The Bhagavad Gita declares, "Perform action without regard for the fruits of action," words as famous in India as they are unattainable.

The only escape route from attachment is the witness. You aren't obliged to set the ego free; it can't be done anyway. By understanding that only the witness brings non-attachment, you have taken the most important step. The witness transcends thinking and feeling, which sounds abstract. The witness transcends the body, which sounds impossible when you see yourself living inside your body. It helps to examine the experience of ecstasy. The word's Greek roots mean "to stand outside oneself," which conveys the joy of being released from mental and physical attachment.

Pause to consider one of the main points of this sutra: You are witnessing in moments when your awareness comes to life. Your true nature is sending you a message about who you really are and what you need to do. Awakening is the doorway to complete spiritual detachment. Being released from every kind of attachment feels like a sacrifice to "I," which bases its existence on wanting, desiring, possessing, and achieving.

In reality there is no sacrifice. You are freeing yourself to discover your true nature, which opens up a truth the separate self never suspected. Experiencing your true nature fulfills all worldly desires. Instead of trying to piece together fulfillment one desire at a time, you have attained the one thing you wanted all along, to be enough in yourself.

The next time you find yourself strongly attached to an outcome—whether it's winning an argument, receiving praise, or achieving a goal—pause and take a deep breath. Instead of resisting your desire or trying to suppress it, ask yourself: "Can I allow this to be as it is?" Release control and feel the space that opens up when you do, even for a moment. A sense of ease arises when you are no longer grasping. Non-attachment isn't about giving up; it's about trusting that who you are is already enough, no matter how things turn out.

Flow is timeless

·

TIME IS A MAJOR CAUSE OF STRESS IN MODERN LIFE—THERE
never seems to be enough of it. With time pressure being such a
common experience, the concept of flow sounds very appealing. Flow
removes time pressure, replacing it with unobstructed movement
from one moment to the next. (Flow brings to mind a river, which in
a poem by William Wordsworth glides on its "own sweet will.")

Effortless action is part of being in the flow, as are calmness and
inner quiet. The contrast with everyday life couldn't be more pro-
nounced; everyone experiences obstacles and resistance that block
the way forward. You can improve things by working through each
obstacle, but what really makes a difference is to realize that flow isn't
like a river at all. Flow isn't in motion, just the opposite. Flow is
changeless. It has nowhere to go, because it is a property of pure consciousness. Even ordinary time is a reflection of consciousness.

Each of us experiences three states of time: time ticking on the
clock when we are awake, time doing strange things in our dreams,
and the absence of time when we're in dreamless sleep. This tells
you that time is tied to your state of consciousness. We take it for
granted that one version of time—the one measured by clocks—is
real time, but that's not true. All three experiences of time—waking,
dreaming, and sleeping—are personal experiences. Your state of
awareness determines what time is. Maya creates the illusion that
time is moving forward as part of the waking dream. When you
are tied to "the arrow of time," as physics calls this forward motion,
you are subject to all the worries about never having enough time.

There is deep fear about what happens when your time finally runs out.

Time has no meaning outside human awareness, not for us at least. But pure consciousness is timeless. The more connected you are to the source, the more your experience of time shifts. Being here now dawns as a possibility, then a real experience, and finally your total experience.

The timeless is with us at every second of our lives. Yet something looks fishy about that sentence, because it makes no sense to say that the timeless is with us "at every second." The timeless has nothing to do with clock time. The timeless is with us, period. There is no need to wait for death or Heaven to prove that eternity is real. On awakening, you realize that the world is timeless in its true nature. Clock time has no privileged position. In fact, some Eastern traditions hold that deep sleep, where there is no clock time, is the most genuine experience of pure consciousness one can have. Right now, you don't experience anything in deep sleep, but to someone who has reached unity consciousness, sleep is experienced for what it really is, a state of awareness as awake as any other. It sounds paradoxical to think about being awake in your sleep, but pure consciousness is at its most vivid when there is nothing mental to block it and no distractions from the outside world.

As Einstein proved, time is relative, but the timeless is absolute. You can't relate to the timeless. You can't accept or reject it. It simply is. The same thing can be said about flow. It is the eternal unfolding of creation. This truth produces a strange situation. As with the saying "Be in the world but not of it," your true self is in time but not of it. Your body ages while your being doesn't. How does being timeless feel? We get a hint in those moments when time stands still. Awe and wonder feel uncanny because the experience of time standing still is so vivid. There's a simpler way to have the same experience, however. In meditation, reaching inner silence makes time stand still. The deeper you go inside yourself, the more at home you feel in the timeless. In unity consciousness, you are there permanently.

Being timeless doesn't mean that you will be late for work or miss your flight at the airport. The history of the universe continues to unfold. Yet behind the scenes, your true nature takes over. As the Indian master Ramana Maharshi puts it, "Time is only an idea. If you do not think you are in time, there will be no time. Find out who you are, and time will take care of itself." That's exactly what people desire from flow.

Even before awakening is reached, the more connected you are to your true nature, the easier your life will be—flow becomes a personal experience without having to do anything external to get there. The flow of creation is neither "in here" nor "out there," because pure consciousness is all-embracing.

Finding Your Wisdom

NO RESISTANCE

Resistance feels like the right response when an experience is unwanted. Your mind pushes back, and many experiences feel like a tug-of-war. Sometimes the thing you resist wins out in the end. The spiritual teaching of putting up no resistance doesn't fit with everyday life, where we push against all kinds of things. Resisting temptation, resisting the impulse to get angry, resisting things that feel wrong—it seems undeniable that resistance has a positive part to play. If you decide for spiritual reasons to stop putting up resistance, the aim is to allow life to flow, but the issue is deeper than it looks.

It is impossible for the mind to know in advance whether or not resistance is appropriate. Waiting until Mr. or Ms. Right says "I love you," we push away opportunities that might blossom into love given enough time. We push away what we fear, losing the opportunity of defeating fear and coming out stronger on the other side. Deciding that you are going to stop resisting doesn't resolve these issues. Acceptance has its own perils. Saying yes to everything can turn out as badly as saying no to everything. Yes loses out whenever it's better to say no, and vice versa.

In the waking dream, acceptance and resistance are paired and inseparable. The play of Maya embraces both, and the more you strive forward against all obstacles, the more obstacles you will experience. An axiom applies here: Whatever you resist, persists.

On the spiritual front, the teaching of non-resistance holds that you should surrender to the flow of life, allowing the natural course of events to unfold. This is the most idealistic approach to saying yes to everything, but it still runs into the same problem—that acceptance and resistance are inexorably joined.

As I'm sure you can foretell, there is a level of life where total non-resistance is not only possible but the most natural way of existing. It is the level where consciousness takes care of every situation. The cell in your body operates without resistance to the unfolding of DNA; there's no other way for hundreds of thousands of different proteins inside a cell to be coordinated. But consciousness is flexible. It accommodates situations where resistance is necessary, as in the face of violence and wrongdoing. In between total acceptance and total resistance, everything is mixed in an unpredictable way.

Awakening allows you to see that the same organizing intelligence that manages trillions of cells in perfect synchronicity applies to creation as a whole. Your true nature has been influencing you since you were born. It has always held out the promise of an ideal life. It's this vision that can guide you to make better choices. Experiences that align with your ideal life should be accepted and embraced; experiences that point in the opposite direction should be resisted.

Attaining the ideal life happens when you are fully awake. In the meantime, trust your true nature whenever it inspires you to be selfless, empathic, self-reliant, flexible, open, and tolerant. These are impulses that feel right, while resistance feels tense, tight, anxious, angry, defiant, stubborn, and rigid—some of these are always present. Paying attention at this level of feeling is infinitely more reliable than trying to think your way through every situation.

True surrender gains everything And sacrifices nothing

•

IN SPIRITUALITY, SURRENDER OPENS THE WAY TO YOUR TRUE nature, which is what awakening is all about. There is everything to gain and nothing to lose. But *surrender* is such a loaded word that the whole issue is clouded. Giving oneself totally to a higher power runs counter to the everyday meaning of *surrender,* which has negative connotations. To be defeated in war means surrender to the enemy. Giving in to a controlling or abusive relationship is a surrender of personal power, accepting the role of victim instead. Surrendering to the police sacrifices your freedom. To make spiritual surrender feel positive, we have to erase those connotations of loss, defeat, and sacrifice.

Spiritual surrender has positive connotations we're all familiar with, especially when a higher divine power is invoked. You can feel how irresistible early Christianity was if you imagine the poor and impoverished hearing Jesus's promise for the first time: "Come to me, all who are weary and burdened . . . learn from me, for I am gentle and humble in heart, and you will find rest for your souls." The words are beautiful, and the promise of surrender to the gentlest of divine beings has been entrancing over the centuries. But the divine presents another face, too. In duality, a benign God is paired with a punishing and threatening God.

Then there is the mystical side of surrender, as when Lao Tzu, the greatest proponent of the Tao, says, "The world is won by those who let it go." This points in the direction of a reality beyond the physical world that imparts enormous power if you surrender to it. But sad experience tells us that the meek didn't inherit the Earth, and power struggles bring ruthlessness, greed, and selfishness to the surface. Anyone who has fallen in love knows the ecstatic feeling of surrendering to the beloved. In everyday life, though, the spell of infatuation is broken. Duality presents many reasons to be unloving instead.

True surrender doesn't happen on any of these levels. The only way is to surrender who you are. You escape the confines of the separate self. The higher power that you surrender to is your true self. Everyone already has glimpses of true surrender. At one end there are courageous acts of self-sacrifice when the ego gives up its innate need for survival. Firemen rushing to save a child in a burning house and soldiers in battle carrying a wounded comrade to safety are inspiring examples. Many children of immigrants carry lifelong gratitude for a selfless mother who worked as a menial laborer, sacrificing everything for the future of her children. The word *selfless* would be better defined as "ego-less." "I" surrenders to a higher value like love and compassion.

These examples, however, don't carry us beyond duality. Surrendering who you are is the only escape route, and this happens only when awareness surrenders to awareness. If we could directly experience the inner lives of those soldiers, firefighters, and mothers, we would see that something greater than "I" has taken over. When higher awareness directs any of us, the communication is immediate and impossible to ignore.

Action in a crisis isn't the same as everyday life, naturally, and we ignore higher awareness all the time in favor of "me" and "mine." Ego can't be eradicated, but it doesn't need to be. True surrender gains everything the ego wants by another means. Fulfillment comes by surrendering who you are in separation for who you are in your essence, your true nature. There's nothing outside you to possess and no prize to win. In and of itself, your true nature is fulfilled. You know you have surrendered when there is no more thought of "I" and "mine." This is one of the primary signs of awakening.

There's a useful exercise that consists of going an entire day without using the word "I." Many fascinating things happen if you try this even for a few hours. To begin with, you've adopted a different, more objective point of view. "I need," "I want," "I think," and "I feel" are out of bounds. You start asking, "Should we?," "What's called for?," or "What does everyone think?" instead. Since your ego finds it so hard to come up with formulations that exclude "I," "me," and "mine," it becomes easier simply to say nothing and to listen to others. You might even find that there's restfulness in rising above your ego, allowing a simple state of awareness to prevail.

In the end, all forms of spiritual surrender amount to the same thing: giving yourself over to being. It is profoundly true that your being is the same as Being itself, the infinite expanse of existence. In Being is the reality of salvation that centuries of seekers have yearned for. Outside the prison of the separate self, the field of Being, existence, and consciousness merge. The highest state of fulfillment arrives here and now.

Finding Your Wisdom

LETTING GO

SURRENDER SOUNDS MORE POSITIVE TO PEOPLE WHEN it is couched as "letting go." Everyone can identify with the misery created by holding on to old grudges, resentments, lost hopes, and cherished dreams that never came true. Unfortunately, learning how to let go is elusive. There's a sticky quality to bad experiences that makes the mind cling to them. It isn't that people find pleasure in reminding themselves over and

over about past hurts, trauma, failure, lost love, and humiliation. Something deeper is at work that needs to be understood
before spiritual surrender becomes possible.

The main enemy of letting go, and the chief obstacle to surrender, is the ego's habit of building a story out of the past. This
habit isn't selective. Good and bad memories are both part of
everyone's story. You can't pick and choose your way through
the past like a grocery shopper squeezing the avocados to get
a ripe one. In other words, we are cooperating with the sticki-
ness of bad memories. On their own, the worst memories
create deep imprints that defy attempts to ignore or forget
them.

To escape this bind, the process of letting go must be
turned on its head. Stuck experiences let go of you, not the
other way around. If you have ever struggled to let go of painful memories, some might be totally forgotten as if they had
never existed while others are almost as painful to recollect as
when they first occurred. What did you do differently to get
such opposite results? Probably nothing. Struggling to let go
is an ego-driven process that has no clear guidelines. "I'm trying to forget" doesn't translate into something you can actually do.

Why do we keep repeating what didn't work in the first
place? Because the ego can't let go. "I" has a self-centered point
of view, and you gain a kind of pseudo-satisfaction from telling
yourself how right you are. Only awareness can change awareness. Understanding this, you can stop fixating on old hurts
and wrongs. Let your higher awareness step in to dissolve the
imprints of painful experiences in the past.

You, the separate self, have to do nothing. What this means
in practical terms is that attention comes to the aid of intention. You have the intention of being released from an unwanted memory. If the memory comes to mind (perhaps you

catch sight of a former friend or lover who has wronged you), notice the feeling that arises as an automatic reflex. Pay attention to it without judgment, simply observing.

Two things will happen. You have stopped feeding your old memory with a resurgence of anger, resentment, self-pity, the desire for revenge, or any other negative emotion. At the same time, the clarity of your attention starts to defuse the stuck energy that unwanted memories feed off.

If you have the opportunity, find a quiet place where you can be alone. Sit with your eyes closed, breathing normally, and observe what happens. If the old memory is too strong, you can stop at any time. It's good to realize that you aren't responsible for letting go. Awareness has healing power over itself—that's the spiritual secret that makes letting go as painless and effortless as possible.

Natural and supernatural are united, You are both

·

THE NATURAL WORLD IS IMMEDIATE AND FAMILIAR, WHILE THE realm of the supernatural, which skeptics don't believe even exists, is beyond everyday experience. Awakening reveals that the natural environment isn't separate and apart from the supernatural environment. You inhabit both domains, fluidly moving between the two as if no boundary existed between them. In reality, there is no boundary. Therefore, if you live in the natural world, you have no choice but to live in the realm of the supernatural. More than this, awakening reveals that you *are* both.

The tendency is to label as "supernatural" anything that defies your worldview. It's one thing for a miracle to occur; it's another for a culture to allow it in. Rejection is the easiest response. From an awakened viewpoint, any phenomenon can manifest from the source. Belief or faith isn't of primary importance. Lowering boundaries that the mind has artificially constructed is. The Vedic tradition in India erected no boundaries, which is why the Yoga sutras, the source of all yogic principles, includes a section on *siddhis,* abilities that include levitation, psychic powers, and the fulfillment of any desire. What seems impossible to most Western minds has a place as "perfections of consciousness" in Yoga.

For a miracle to be real, it must be real *for you.* In an age of faith, miracles are real, and evidence of divine grace, but are subject to rational dismissal in the modern secular world. The reverse can also happen when people who know nothing about science are exposed to an everyday occurrence that for them becomes miraculous. A vivid confirmation of this occurred in World War II with the "cargo cults" in Melanesia. Allied forces set up military bases on various Pacific islands. The local Indigenous populations, who had limited prior contact with industrialized societies, witnessed soldiers receiving large quantities of supplies—referred to as "cargo"—from planes and ships. These supplies included food, clothing, weapons, and other goods.

The Indigenous people, observing this influx of material wealth and unfamiliar technology, developed the belief that these goods were sent by ancestral spirits or deities. Some interpreted the Allied soldiers as intermediaries who had discovered the "correct" rituals or behaviors to summon these valuable goods.

Miracles never lose their allure, and verified miracles, including the seventy-two miraculous cures at Lourdes, are accepted by the Catholic Church; these are vastly outnumbered by reports of miracles throughout the Catholic world. Miracles are required for a saint to be recognized. But the wonder felt when contemplating a miracle doesn't lower the boundary between the natural and the supernatural.

What's needed is to set aside all worldviews. Skeptics and believers alike are doing the same thing, indulging in confirmation bias. A stage magician who can duplicate the feats of psychics and spoon-benders hasn't disproven their validity; offering an imitation isn't the same as refutation. A report of levitation without an unfaked video lends no credence to a mind wedded to materialism. Something very different happens, however, when awakening removes the bias of a worldview.

Seen clearly, the natural world, beginning with our own physical bodies, is actually inexplicable. No one has any idea how the brain converts invisible photons into visible light, particularly considering that there is only darkness in the visual cortex. Brain scans can follow the most precise patterns of neural activity associated with thinking, but total ignorance is encountered if you ask how silent brain cells create a voice in your head. There is no science capable of describing the pre-created state before the Big Bang, or how this timeless, formless, inconceivable domain managed to perfectly synchronize time, space, matter, and energy.

There's a baffling contradiction between the randomness that supposedly rules in Nature; the laws of chemistry and physics, which are the opposite of random; and the spectacle that meets our eyes of a living world constructed in elaborate forms of beauty and intricacy. Everyone knows the famous hypothesis that, given enough time, monkeys tapping randomly on typewriters would eventually produce the complete works of Shakespeare. Using advanced computer modeling, this claim has been debunked.

In a fanciful test, British researchers in 2003 placed a typewriter in the monkey house of the Paignton Zoo. The reported results were "five pages of text, primarily filled with the letter S." Early trials with randomized computer programs did yield intelligible words and even phrases. Now the most sophisticated statistical study to date has concluded that "there is simply not enough time until the universe expires for a defined number of hypothetical primates to produce a faithful reproduction of *Curious George,* let alone *King Lear.*" The odds of a monkey typing out the first phrase of Hamlet's "To be or not to be" on a thirty-key keyboard were 1 in 900.

Yet Darwinian theory holds that mutations occurring just as randomly as a monkey's strokes on a keyboard are the basis of the 3 billion base pairs in human DNA, from which all genetic functions derive. DNA as organized in the human genome carries not just the code of life but the meaningful function performed by every cell. Our bodies are an expression of billions of genetic words, so to speak. (By comparison, Shakespeare's plays contain 844,000 words in all.) The path that leads from a random mutation to the limitless intelligence embodied in the human brain feels suspect. Meaningless events don't suddenly acquire meaning by a wave of the hand. The intelligence in human DNA isn't restricted to the construction of our DNA. DNA is intelligence in action, organizing and overseeing tens of thousands of processes simultaneously in every cell. This is accomplished nearly perfectly, but when DNA divides in half to create a new cell, chemical monitors slide up and down the helix to spot and repair defects.

Arguing about whether a cell is natural or supernatural is a mind-made issue. Some processes in Nature seem to be blindly mechanical, as when hydrogen bonds with oxygen to form water. Others, like the existence of consciousness, have no rational explanation—existence comes packaged with awareness. No prior process created it. The primary quality of consciousness is creative intelligence, which human beings have used to create every civilization. As a property of consciousness, creative intelligence also cannot be explained through any prior process.

Even without awakening, these facts are inarguable. Nature and supernature are one whole. You have a right to point to any feature in creation and say, "I am that." Once this realization sinks in, the mind-made boundary between the natural and the supernatural collapses.

Finding Your Wisdom

IRRATIONAL IMPULSES

WE WRONGLY ELEVATE RATIONALITY AS IF IT OPENED AN ideal path for human behavior. It is just as mistaken to treat the irrational like the enemy of reason. In the state of separation, you can't have one without the other. Seen clearly, reason and unreason present an impossible choice. Mathematics is the crown jewel of rational logic, but love is the crown jewel of emotional fulfillment. Our worst irrational impulses lead to war, but science, which prides itself on being rational, created nuclear bombs, lethal biochemicals, and the horror of weapons of mass destruction.

Everyday life is caught in the same impossible choice. On

the path to awakening, this becomes crystal clear. Most people hide their irrational side behind a thin veneer of reason, particularly when making important or life-changing decisions. All such decisions are driven by two forces—a desire to get something good and a fear of things not working out. Small choices aren't much better. They are either harmless, like choosing what to wear in the morning, or habitual, like choosing which foods you like or dislike.

None of this could be called an exercise in rationality. That's not a criticism. The irrational impulses that actually motivate people are invaluable. It is irrational to sit down and write a poem or compose a symphony. If the poem or symphony is great, we attribute that to inspiration, which is purely an irrational force yet cherished nonetheless. But the highest achievements of humanity don't mitigate hatred, violence, and fear—the demons of irrationality. We abhor those impulses in others and struggle to suppress them in ourselves. Without realizing it, many people adhere to Freud's view that civilization exists to tamp down the dark forces that lurk deep within us.

Awakening presents an entirely different model. Setting aside everything you think about the worst and best in human nature, the reality is that best and worst are expressions of consciousness. Your true nature gives you infinite choices. These choices exist before anything else happens. The fact that we can choose rationality is primary. What we do with rationality is secondary.

The same is true of our irrational behavior. We have free choice over our behavior in consciousness. The outcome is secondary. At first glance this doesn't seem to solve anything. The worst irrational choices exist in awareness, just as the best choices do. The difference lies in processing, and it's a huge difference. Anger, fear, and violence are the outcomes of psychological processing. They emerge from a tangle of causes that might include childhood abuse (which Hitler and Stalin were both subjected to); a history of animosity between tribes, religions, and nations; the absence of love; poor social adjustment; low self-esteem; lack of acceptance by peers; and much else.

Psychological processing occurs in the mind in its incessant activity. Awareness isn't like this—it is the field of possibilities, like the blank canvas a painter faces before choosing the first daub of color. You can't predict what the final painting will be, but a genuine artist is guided by love of beauty and a great artist by inspiration. Those impulses come from closer to the source; they are expressions of our true nature.

You can demonstrate this to yourself. Pick a person or thing you strongly dislike and ask yourself why you feel that way. Let your mind freely offer reasons. Whatever it comes up with, notice that your dislike has a history. Some cause or string of causes lies behind your animosity. Now think of someone or something you love. If you pay attention, you will notice that love needs no cause or history. It arises as a spontaneous impulse. The same is true of something you find beautiful. Its beauty strikes you immediately. In other words, the impulses we hold in the highest esteem arise closer to our true nature while the impulses we decry arise through mental processing.

Once you notice the difference, you can reframe irrationality in the most positive terms, as the source of beauty, love, truth, inspiration, and creativity. At the same time, discard any judgment against the irrational. Without it, you can't be fully human.

The ideal life is an arc Of expanding awareness

•

A T ANY TIME FROM BIRTH ONWARD, YOU ARE DESIGNED FOR expanding awareness. This is a constant as innate as breathing. No cut-off point exists in the journey, which is shaped as a rising arc. That the oldest among us should be wise follows this arc. The expansion of awareness has milestones along the way that are points of arrival, one following the other, until full awakening dawns. But it is the naturalness of the process that most strikingly makes this path different. No other way of fulfilling your potential compares. What truly matters is the never-ending story written in consciousness.

Because *Homo sapiens* is defined by two unique physical traits, our higher brain and our DNA, our tremendous potential has been explained scientifically by focusing on them. Brain activity and the expression of your genes aren't primary, however. The physical setup follows along, mirroring awareness—as we saw, your body, including your brain and your DNA, is the vehicle for consciousness to emerge in the world.

The expansion of awareness is necessary, as reflected by brain development. By a quirk of evolution, birth occurs after nine months, but the infant brain isn't fully developed yet. It is already enormously complex in the womb, growing millions of neurons every day in the third trimester—too many, in fact—but not yet fully organized, which accounts for the helplessness of newborns. (We are the opposite of Arctic caribou, whose newborns are ready to walk and follow the wandering herd within a few minutes after emerging from the womb.)

The situation requires a human baby's brain to keep developing after birth. In a spurt of furious activity, the brain of a newborn infant consumes approximately 60 percent of the body's daily energy requirements; the adult brain uses only 20 percent. Other species are estimated to devote around 2.8 percent of their metabolic energy to the brain. The needless surplus of brain cells is reduced to a functional number while the baby's first experiences organize all their necessary functions, like focused eyesight and recognition of their mother.

However, all this pales in significance when set beside the fact, unique in Nature, that the human brain isn't considered fully mature until one's early to mid-twenties. In 1900 the average life expectancy in the United States was between forty-six and forty-eight years, so almost half a lifetime was spent simply achieving adulthood (for Black men, who lived on average thirty-two to thirty-three years, an adult barely had enough time to be an adult).

What was awareness doing all this time? The brain has the advantage that neuroscience can see and measure it, unlike expanding awareness, which is invisible and eludes measurement. Yet despite the enormous attention paid to the brain, awareness was actually performing the most vital part of the process. It creates meaning and purpose. It provides an identity. Experiences get sorted out and remembered as part of a person's story. It has never been shown in the slightest that neurons are capable of any of these things.

If you were born awakened, there would be no question about the primacy of consciousness. Being born would be the instant realization of "I am." You would spontaneously understand that the five senses, viewed as brain functions, can't possibly create sights, sounds, textures, tastes, and smells, none of which exist in the silent, dark brain. But awakening doesn't happen at birth, which introduces the necessity of expanding your awareness through every phase that precedes awakening. Those phases include learning to walk, speak, write, and reason. DNA guides some of those processes and participates in the others.

The fully mature brain of a twenty-two-year-old surrenders its dominant role up to that point. It has mirrored every step of physical and mental development in a rising arc since birth. What lies ahead is the rising arc of self-awareness. It has no biological function; those have been taken care of and are now in place. Self-awareness is totally voluntary and happens "in here" without external triggers.

Seen clearly, self-awareness is disconnected from ego, personality, IQ, social standing, and personal relationships. These qualities move along in a zigzag, up-and-down path. For this very reason, the Bhagavad Gita declares that there are no outward signs of enlightenment. Only awareness can relate to awareness.

The rising arc that occurs in awareness is the ultimate example of free will, not by what you choose to do with your life but by choosing to pay attention. Countless people have no idea how critical that choice is. Fortunately, human awareness is designed to experience the rising arc. Anyone can begin to pay attention at any time, and then the ideal life begins to reveal itself, exactly as we are designed for.

Finding Your Wisdom

PAYING ATTENTION

IF YOU DON'T PAY ATTENTION TO IT, AWARENESS WON'T draw attention to itself. By comparison, the ego and the mind are great show-offs. They can't help themselves. "I" is preoccupied with a daily stream of desires, duties, and demands. The mind is preoccupied with feeling, thinking, and sensing. Those are the things we inevitably pay attention to. Awakening doesn't depend on paying attention in the ordinary way, though. Despite the attractions of endless experiences in the world and the potential for fascinating thoughts, only one kind of attention leads to awakening: awareness paying attention to itself.

A movie screen makes for a useful comparison. No matter how many images are cast on the screen, it remains unchanged, not touched by drama, comedy, or tragedy. I've used this analogy for how unchanged and untouched pure consciousness is, but analogies can take us only so far. A movie screen doesn't watch the movie. Awareness is always watching, and apart from anything that happens "out there" or "in here," awareness watches itself.

It is understandable and totally forgivable that the thinking mind can't grasp how this works. The mind must have something to look at or think about. Otherwise, it would be like a computer with no software to run it, a kind of dead space. But the space that the mind occupies (*Chit Akash* in Sanskrit) is vibrantly alive, alert, dynamic, and self-aware. A computer is useless until it performs a task. Consciousness needs no tasks; it is fulfilled without anything to see or think about.

This state of freedom you can sense by paying attention. In meditation or simply in a moment of calm, your awareness has no burdens, memories, pressing thoughts, or emotions. The absence of those things is like blowing dust off a mirror. Your awareness reflects itself in silence with a simplicity that is liberating. Being here in the present moment with nothing to occupy you is also freeing. In the tradition of Gyan Yoga, which works to awaken the mind, taking away every distraction is critical.

Like clearing away a cluttered attic, you look at everything that obscures pure awareness, responding with "Not this, not that" (known in Sanskrit as *Neti Neti*). This path is typically considered intellectual. The yogi examines all the words and concepts that do not pertain to pure consciousness, of which there is a long list: birth, death, cause and effect, beginning and ending, boundaries, limitations, time, space, physical objects, thoughts, feelings, religious beliefs—anything the thinking mind can conceive of when it looks around at the world of Maya.

But "not this, not that" doesn't have to be intellectual; it is extremely difficult to get the thinking mind to give up. There is an intuitive sense that tells us when an experience is what we are looking for. After a lifetime of thinking and feeling, it is obvious on the intuitive level that no experience has led to awakening. The whole activity of the mind can be seen immediately as "not this."

It isn't so obvious on the intuitive level, however, that the mind is being pulled toward the source. Your mind knows what it is like to be fulfilled by a satisfying meal or a personal achievement, and it is these bits and pieces we hope to string together to achieve greater, lasting fulfillment. What has developed is the habit of needing an experience of X to give us a moment of fulfillment. Take away X, and the mind fears a vacuum. In reality, the most satisfying experience you have stored away in your box of beautiful recollections is a means to an end.

The end is fulfillment, pure and simple. Because awareness is fulfilled in itself, no X intrudes—even a painful experience doesn't disturb you in full awakening. This isn't numbness, denial, delusion, or willpower. "Not this, not that" has gotten its message through. Wake up to your true nature, and you don't need a means to an end. You have arrived at the end and fully inhabit it. This description may sound abstract, but by resting in awareness without distraction, you've found the right path.

The evolution of consciousness Is what makes us human

•

THE DRIVING FORCE BEHIND CREATION IS EVOLUTION, WHICH governs on a cosmic scale as well as at the level of the most primitive one-celled organisms on Earth. If you had a convenient time machine and traveled back tens of millions of years, the creatures you'd encounter would give no hint of future evolutionary transformations. The living world looks stable at every age, yet the force of evolution *is* transformation.

The appearance of permanence is misleading. Creatures come and go in waves of extinction—scientists estimate that at least 99.9 percent of all species of plants and animals that ever lived are extinct. At least half of all species that look like evolutionary winners die out in a short period of time. How could evolution prevail over the randomness of such wanton destruction? Even genetic mutations obey the statistical laws of random distribution. At birth, you, like every baby, had around sixty or seventy new genetic variants that are not present in your parents' chromosomes. Some of these mutations might be harmless, like a slight change in the gene for eye color, but others could have significant effects. For example, a mutation might make you more resistant to a particular disease, or it could result in a stronger bone structure, improving your chance of not suffering bone thinning as you age.

The coexistence of randomness and evolution demands an explanation, and leaning on randomness alone, as Darwinism does, isn't sufficient. Order finds a way to emerge, not by steps of physical mutation but all at once. For example, there is no precedent for the emergence of logic, reason, and mathematics in any primate except us. The last frontier for evolution is awareness, whose creativity is infinite, while the physical building blocks of brain and body are basically just a handful of ordinary organic chemicals that build every other living thing. To know what is really happening, evolution must be revealed behind the mask of matter.

Think of a great painting you love, such as one by the Impressionists. If you were the proverbial alien who has just landed on Earth in a spaceship, paintings might be unknown to you. The alien might ask you how such a thing came about.

His confusion wouldn't be helped if you started to explain what a painting was by holding up a painter's palette, loaded with colors. The jumble displays no hint of the finished picture. Confusion would only deepen if you started daubing brushstrokes at random on a blank canvas. What would the alien think if you explained that an invisible force, known as inspiration, guided the great painter's hand and that behind inspiration lay abstract thought, behind thought something known as awareness, which isn't even a thought?

No matter where you begin, any creation made by human beings—a painting, a house, a car, or an entire city—follows a path tracing the visible and tangible back through layers of invisible, intangible processes. Even if you pause at the brain in your explanation, pointing to it as the root cause of Impressionism, it's unlikely that the alien would understand how a mushy mass of gray matter, devoid of light or images, could produce a Monet painting of the shimmering Rouen Cathedral at dawn.

All of us comfortably inhabit the levels of consciousness that make creativity possible. You effortlessly process the world through the domains of awareness known in ancient India: mind (*manas* in Sanskrit), intellect (*buddhi*), ego (*ahankara*), memory and the subconscious (*chit*), and pure self-awareness (*atman*). In Yoga and Vedanta there are many finer distinctions, but a simple point arises even from the basic map just given: Each level of awareness is coordinated with every other. That's the secret allowing us to freely move in and out of every level. As evidence of creative evolution, this ability is powerful.

Just as only awareness can be aware, only creativity can be creative. That's how randomness is overcome. Like the random daubs of paint that resolve into a finished painting of Rouen Cathedral, evolution leads to a finished goal, whether a tiger, a minnow, or a fern, through a concept that was complete to begin with. The source drives creation from one finished thing to the next. If you watched an embryo in the womb under a microscope, you'd see nothing but random movement inside every cell, but trillions of molecular steps unfold into the perfect orderliness of a baby. The future was determined at the instant of conception. T. S. Eliot's famous line, "In the end is my beginning," applies to evolution.

Without this feature, disorder would have wiped out evolution long ago. Human DNA has billions of parts, which gives billions of chances for the double helix to go haywire. On a cosmic scale, every element heavier than iron came to Earth as interstellar dust from exploding supernovae millions of light-years away. Dust has every chance to be nothing but dusty, yet it created the natural world, and us, here on Earth. If that dust had far more radioactive elements in it, like uranium and plutonium, it would have meant curtains for life on Earth as we know it.

What awakening reveals, in a word, is that evolution is creative because it occurs in consciousness. A Monet cathedral obviously began in the artist's consciousness, whether you insert the brain into the process or not. The mask of matter that cloaks creation exists everywhere you look, but seeing beyond the mask is the whole point of awakening.

Finding Your Wisdom

LIVING CREATIVELY

LIVING YOUR LIFE CREATIVELY ISN'T ABOUT HAVING artistic or musical talent. It's about the evolution of consciousness, which has taken you to the point where you find yourself now. You have made choices that align with evolution, and these have had positive effects. But because society doesn't teach us about how consciousness evolves, you have also made non-evolutionary choices that have not turned out the way you hoped. This is a better way to describe how a person's life unfolds than talking about good and bad choices.

Good and bad choices are tied to their outcome, and outcomes are often unforeseen—you can't predict from meeting someone for the first time whether a relationship will develop, and, if so, how much happiness or pain will ensue. Evolutionary choices, on the other hand, are knowable from the outset, and, more important, how they will turn out is predetermined. By analogy, when you throw a ball, the instant it leaves your hand, the ball's trajectory is set. There is no gap between letting the ball fly and where it finally lands.

If you pause to consider, the phenomenon of "in the beginning is the end" rules Nature. In a healthy pregnancy, there is no gap between conception and birth. All creatures are born through the working out of genes. For them, biology is destiny. An aardvark has no choice but to be an aardvark in body, behavior, instincts, diet, mating habits, and everything else that comprises the complete finished state of the creature.

Human completeness is unique in our ability to evolve "de novo," the term applied when something new appears without precedent. The sixty to seventy new genetic variants that you possess, none of which came as an inheritance from your parents, are "de novo" creations. The very fact that you can taste the saltiness of salt and the sweetness of sugar goes back to an unknowable time when those experiences emerged in ancestral hominids. Other creatures need salt, but they aren't aware of saltiness as a conscious experience (as far as we know).

Life is lived creatively when you allow "de novo" free rein. That's how you encourage something new to emerge, like the wetness of water, which has no precedent in oxygen and hydrogen, the two gases in H_2O. Water is defined, in fact, by everything that has nothing to do with gases—liquidity, the way water dissolves almost anything, its habit of flowing downhill, and its ability to be transformed into steam, ice, hail, sleet, and snow. This combination of traits would be unimaginable if water didn't exist. "De novo" creates things that are unique but also fashioned to complete the picture of life on Earth. If water had every quality I listed but was also corrosive or poisonous, it would be an enemy of life instead of a necessity.

As you experience yourself right now, you cannot predict what could emerge "de novo" from you. Anything you can predict simply reshuffles the past. Picasso's father, who was also a painter, made his living producing popular images of doves, a reshuffling of the same image that has no resemblance to his son's endless creativity. But you are already in the "de novo" business, because your next thought comes out of the blue and has every chance of being unique.

It's your choice to align yourself with your source and its infinite creative potential. Alignment is made possible by the fact that you already can freely navigate the levels of awareness labeled as mind, intellect, ego, memory, and pure awareness. Every journey in awareness needs no planning in advance. Being open in your attitude is enough. Your consciousness is designed to evolve, and if you pay attention, you will notice the new things that arise to fascinate you. *Make it new* is the motto of living creatively, and the deeper awareness inside you listens if you have that intention.

See yourself as the conduit through which creative intelligence finds expression in the world. If you pay close attention, you will notice that in every situation there comes a pivot point. You can automatically follow a reflex that is familiar to you or you can turn instead to the unknown, a response that points to a new outcome.

This pivot point is like a fingerpost at a junction, but the two roads it points to aren't physical. They are diverging timelines. The instant you choose to let a new response rise inside your awareness, a different timeline is created. Where it will lead, you can't know in advance. But the promise of evolution is that the destination is written into the inception.

Based on this promise, every intention that has already led to positive outcomes was founded. Awakening simply explains how it worked.

The whole has nothing to do With the sum of its parts

•

WHOLENESS IS MYSTERIOUS FROM BOTH SIDES OF THE FENCE. In the state of separation, you can't be whole, and on awakening, you discover that you already are whole. In either case, despite being opposite, the same conclusion holds true: If you try to become whole, you will be frustrated. The setup of the waking dream, by its very nature, is fragmented. Saying that the whole is greater than the sum of its parts is workable if you mean a house being greater than the sum of its bricks. But it's unworkable to define all kinds of things by examining their parts, counting them up, and deciding that you understand the whole.

In countless ways, your wholeness has nothing to do with the sum of your parts. Consider something as basic as moving your hand. The materials that make up a hand (bones, tendons, skin, nerves, blood vessels, and so on) are designed for maximum mobility, and the impulses from the brain that cause motor reflexes are well-known. All this information is relevant to your physiology, but not to how you actually move your hand.

Moving your hand is a pure expression of consciousness. Since consciousness is infinite, so is your hand's capability. Every created thing in the world—every artifact of art, civilization, science, and technology—required someone's hands to conform to the desire of the mind. As long as music continues to be written, to take a single example, the hands of pianists and violinists will move in new ways without limit. The infinite capacity of your hand points to a larger truth: Wholeness is always infinite. This applies to you in countless ways. There is no limit to what you say, think, and do. We're not talking about counting a lifetime's worth of thoughts, actions, and words. Wholeness is about two things only: potential and manifestation. Consciousness is a field of infinite potential, and when pure consciousness goes into creative mode, what it manifests is also infinite.

Science is so thoroughly in our blood now that measuring and counting dominate Everything. What are your vital signs? How is your cholesterol level? How much has the trade deficit swollen? How big is our atomic weapons stockpile? These statistics and countless more impinge on everyone's life. They are meant to get us somewhere: healthy vital signs, lower cholesterol, a smaller trade deficit, and so on.

Yet by some trick, all this counting and measuring doesn't achieve the right ends. The epidemic of obesity is out of control despite some recent incremental declines. Trade deficits never or rarely go down. Peace isn't achieved through stockpiled weapons. Shifting the view to someone's personal life, counting and measuring don't help us achieve love, happiness, inner fulfillment, truth, creativity, spiritual experiences, or awakening.

Those things are irreducible. They aren't assembled from building blocks. There are no measurable ingredients that lead to a completed recipe, like baking a cake. I'm not discounting the value of things that can be counted, like salary, the size of a house, how large a family is, how much debt is accumulated on credit cards. Daily schedules run by the hour, sometimes by the minute. All of this must be attended to in an orderly, organized life.

Yet if you organized your life perfectly, which is the ideal many people set for themselves, wanting no flaw or blemish, nothing short of the best, and so on, you would find yourself no closer to awakening. You are highly unlikely to attain the qualities of awareness just listed: love, happiness, inner fulfillment, truth, creativity, and spiritual experiences. We don't have to be lofty—you are also unlikely to attain something as mundane as maturity, contentment, self-worth, or feeling up to life's challenges.

Gather all of this together, and another truth emerges: Wholeness gives you your true self. Fragments can't do this. The play of opposites defines Maya. In a subtle way, that's how counting and measuring started. Faced with the natural world, early humans began to sort everything out and put it in its proper place. The earliest cave paintings from 30,000 to 50,000 years ago are marvels of art, but the animals being portrayed are also an inventory of the creatures our ancestors hunted. There are Indigenous people who don't use numbers or they count no higher than four or five. They have existed that way for thousands of years without the trappings of worldliness. Who can say that their experience of love is less powerful than ours or their rates of depression, anxiety, and loneliness higher than ours?

A mania for counting and measuring is the foundation for organizing the world into packages of information. Caught up in this mania, we can pride ourselves on science and technology without seeing that we have cut ourselves off from our true nature and the existence of the true self. To be awakened is to realize that we have been organizing a dream all along. More than that, we have reinforced the dream's hold over us. Maya's setup is so detailed that an unending supply of data can be gathered and computed. This fact is one of the main reasons a skeptic would deny that an illusion exists at all.

But even in normal dreaming, when you're asleep, you can be chased down the street by one person or an army—numbers don't change the fact that it's all dream-stuff. Maya is much more stable than a nightmare about being chased down the street, but the mountain of data that keeps piling up is still part of the illusion. A trillion bits of data, or a trillion trillion, have nothing to do with the whole. Wholeness is a state of awareness, untouched by counting and measuring.

Finding Your Wisdom

ONENESS

EVERYONE SENSES WITHOUT TALKING ABOUT IT THAT we live in the state of separation. As evidence, there is the number one. It divides a person from everyone else: There is only one *you*, but this unique self feels insignificant and vulnerable in its aloneness. "I am only one person" is an expression of powerlessness. The difference between being someone and no one matters in society. If you are competitive, you are driven by the belief that there can be only one winner, and you want to be that one. (A cold war anecdote was told about a Soviet sports story concerning a race where only Russia and the United States competed. The United States won, and supposedly the Russian newspapers reported this as "Russia came in second, but America came in next to last.")

The more you reflect, the more it seems that the number one is critical to how we live in separation. Looking out for number one is like a credo for some people, yet even the most modest person doesn't want to feel second-rate. A celebrity in the room is the one all eyes are fixed upon. As commonplace as these examples might be, they disguise the reality of who you are because, if you look closely, you don't see yourself as either no one or someone.

The basic feeling of "I am" isn't attached to a number, not even the number one. "I am" is an all-pervasive experience that has no boundaries. As long as you are in a physical body, existence is a given. The state of separation overlooks this fundamental fact, assigning it little importance. Awakening reveals that existence is also conscious, at which point "I am" is filled with infinite potential in and of itself.

Oneness describes your relationship to awareness here and now. You are at one with pure consciousness. This realization erases all the connotations of one as a number, both positive and negative. Seeing yourself in the state of oneness doesn't require awakening. Oneness has a practical side. Your heart beats without counting how many times it beats, and the same is true for your respiratory system. Those processes are continuous, as are the processes that build and maintain every cell. Life, in other words, is one thing, even though we cut it up into slices for the purposes of science and medicine.

If you unfold the state of oneness into its key elements, you get the following:

I am at one with myself.
I am a continuity, not a sequence of separate thoughts, words, and deeds.
My existence is unbounded, since "I am" is borderless.
I am at one with my awareness, and my awareness is immersed in existence.
There is no difference between my sense of "I am" and the same sense felt by all people.

Awakening makes each of these statements self-evident. Yet even on the path to awakening, if you let them sink in, these elements already define you. Oneness is your birthright and ultimately your true identity.

Mysticism has a special place In the deeper reality

•

WHEN SOMETHING IS TOTALLY BEYOND EXPLANATION, WE call it a mystery, and the department where mysteries are gathered is mysticism. If you are highly rational, particularly if you put your complete faith in science, you never open the door to the department of mysticism. You know in advance that it is a rubbish closet. Everything in it can be discarded, along with superstition and mythology, as the products of ignorance. But there's always another perspective, and from the perspective of awakening, mysticism is totally necessary. When nothing else works, it serves as the explanation of last resort.

Reality can't be explained without leaving some crucial matters as mysteries. What preceded the Big Bang is a total mystery, for example, and when a theory is offered, such as the multiverse, it is an explanation of last resort—it has to be. There is no other choice, because human explanations exist in time and space, and whatever came before the Big Bang can't be measured in terms of time and space.

That's an example of mysticism arising because the human brain isn't equipped physically to reach into the unknown. But mysticism can be homegrown and personal. No one can explain what a thought is or how visual images appear in the totally dark recesses of the brain. Everyone takes these phenomena for granted, and if pressed to give an explanation, a shrug of the shoulders is the likely answer.

Such mysteries belong in the category of a black box. A black box is a gap between cause and effect. In the case of the brain, the cause is genetic—your brain emerged from the operations of DNA in the womb—and the effect is thoughts and visual images. What happens in between is inexplicable; it is happening as if in a black box no one can look inside of.

It might seem contradictory to insist, "This isn't mysticism." To most people, higher consciousness is nothing but mysterious. Yet consciousness isn't mystical in itself. It's a given, along with existence, and inner exploration reveals how consciousness works, stripping away its mysterious aura. What this leaves untouched, however, are the most fascinating mysteries, those for which mysticism is and always will be the explanation of last resort.

Mention of these mysteries has cropped up here and there, but we can gather them together, as follows:

Higher consciousness is an aspect of human nature.
Your higher consciousness is aware of you even if you aren't aware of it.
Creation is organized and governed from an invisible source.
The material world masks the flow of creative intelligence that constantly pours from the source.
The thinking mind cannot explain what consciousness is or where it comes from.

Awakening does many things, but it doesn't explain any of these. They are mystical because there is no way to get beyond them to find out what makes them true. Yet without these mysteries, human existence would be impossible. The most basic experience of awareness, "I am," can't be lifted above the category of mysticism.

Awakening doesn't abolish mystery, then. It brings you closer to seeing how pervasively mystery touches your existence. The world's most prominent mystics are comfortable with what their inner eye sees.

Some, like Julian of Norwich, are known for being in bliss consciousness: "The fullness of joy is to behold God in everything."

Some, like Meister Eckhart, are known for metaphysical pronouncements: "A free mind has the power to achieve all things."

A few are scientists like the physicist Freeman Dyson, peering into metaphysics: "God is what mind becomes when it passes the threshold of our comprehension."

A genuine mystic speaks as naturally about mysteries as we do about everyday reality, not to solve the mysteries but to acknowledge that they exist. In the state of separation, even this step is often blocked. Duality forces us to make either/or choices about placing our full attention on the physical world or on a world beyond. But there aren't two worlds, just an artificial boundary created by the mind.

There are mysteries that appear to be useful or useless, depending on your perspective. The doctrine of karma, for example, is based on the belief that the universe is morally balanced, so that bad and good actions lead to inexorable results beyond our control. The redress of balance extends across lifetimes, which brings in a second mystery—reincarnation. No matter how objectively the doctrine of karma might be approached, its foundation is a total mystery—no one can predict the consequence of every action or how the goodness or badness of an action is calculated by some higher consciousness with God-like omniscience about every human action.

The biggest question is whether Maya is a genuine mystery or a mystical notion with no basis except its religious roots in Hinduism and earlier. In that tradition, Maya is personified as the goddess of illusion. Yet her personification is unnecessary; what is totally necessary is an explanation of how physical creation automatically led to duality. There the genuine mystery lies. No one is born awake; everyone accepts their participation in the collective waking dream. If the tradition of Maya didn't exist, something would have to take its place. Otherwise, the waking dream would be taken at face value and awakening wouldn't be possible.

But awakening does exist, and, as the explanation of last resort, Maya is useful to describe what we are awakening from.

Finding Your Wisdom

PROVIDENCE

AN IMPERISHABLE IDEA THAT HAS SURVIVED IN EVERY culture is the notion that a higher power is looking down upon human affairs. If a higher power exists, does it take a benign view of us, or one of total indifference? The benign view is known as Providence, whose root is the verb "to provide." Divine Providence, if you believe in it, provides everything necessary for human existence. It answers prayers and furthers our cherished goals. Outside the domain of religion, a belief in a higher power that sides with human beings has a long tradition.

Modern people are still open to the idea. For example, many believe in the power of commitment. The essence of this belief is that once you decide to undertake a challenge, "all sorts of things occur to help one that would never otherwise have occurred." (This quote is from a book on climbing the Himalayas, by the Scottish mountaineer and writer W. H. Murray.) The same belief is echoed in phrases about "invisible forces" or "providence" moving to support decisions of courage and commitment.

If you believe, even casually, that everything happens for a reason, which countless people say, you are connecting the two worlds of "in here" and "out there." An intelligence outside yourself is listening in on the events of your life and trying to let you know that you are heard, seen, and understood. That, too, is part of the awakened life.

Murray had a religious view of the invisible forces that come to aid human beings: "The moment one definitely commits oneself, then Providence moves too." The same reassurance doesn't have to come from a religious source. In his worldwide bestseller *The Alchemist,* Paulo Coelho writes, "When you want something, all the universe conspires in helping you to achieve it." Coelho's source could easily have been Ralph Waldo Emerson using almost the same words more than a hundred years earlier: "Once you make a decision, the universe conspires to make it happen."

Awakening brings a different perspective. The mystery of a higher power supporting your intentions must bow to a more intimate mystery. Why do everyday, commonplace intentions come true? When you have the intention to speak, move your arm, or take your car to the grocery store, an invisible force is at work without rational explanation. Your impulse simply carries itself out. Saying a word is more complex than you might suppose: It involves remembering how to speak in terms of the mechanics of lips, tongue, and vocal cords; you must retrieve the word that matches your meaning; this requires dipping into a vocabulary whose location is totally unknown; and the brain functions required to organize these elements must be instantaneously meshed with other brain areas. As with so much of the brain's activity, signals seem to know where they need to go in advance of going there.

Explaining how a trip to the grocery store works, a much more complicated venture, brings in other mysteries. How do you keep in mind what you are going to buy? You don't repeatedly think about it on the way to the store; when you arrive you recall specific items without knowing how recall works or what you do to trigger it; the mechanics of driving your car are compartmentalized together in a set of automatically coordinated motor skills, including focused eyesight, specific attention to traffic, and a knowledge of the rules of the road that functions without consciously calling them up.

The point is that the mind cannot do without its share of mysticism. We depend on invisible forces beyond our ability to explain them. Providence feels completely real to some people, fictitious to other people, and a matter of indifference to everyone else. It might be that belief creates the phenomenon or vice versa. If enough good things happen to you out of the blue, Providence is as good an explanation as any. Ultimately, Providence belongs in the privileged class of mysteries that are essential to being human. You can pick and choose which mysteries interest you, but you cannot do without.

Awakening brings the end of fear

•

A WAKENING SHOWS HOW UNNECESSARY FEAR IS. THIS REAL-ization applies to everyone. Someone who has awakened no longer feels any fear—of physical harm, disease, violence, or death. Knowing this in advance greatly adds to the appeal of awakening, but you don't have to wake up to get your mind to stop believing in fear. It is this belief that keeps fear as a constant threat in the waking dream.

The beauty of full awakening is expressed by the revered Buddhist monk Thich Nhat Hanh: "Fearlessness is not only possible, it is the ultimate joy. When you touch non-fear, you are free." But the path to bringing the end of fear can begin almost anywhere, from a state of low-level nagging worry to crippling phobias. We have expanded fear to enormous proportions. The overwhelming fear in an age of faith—fearing the wrath of God and the prospect of Hell—has waned in the modern secular world, but humanity rushed in to fill the vacuum. Atomic annihilation is a horror we've learned to live with, and the irony is that the arms race is conducted on the rationale that only a strong defense makes a nation fearless. No, we fear the weapons of defense and cannot find a way to do without them, which means that fear will be ever-present.

It can't be denied that fear is woven into the complexity of our lives. There is a Darwinian argument for fear being an evolutionary advantage—the fight-or-flight response is the most common example. Yet if you experience fight-or-flight, which is triggered by stress hormones, you aren't likely to have time to be afraid. The whole process is physiological, not mental. As a protection against danger, fear is largely unreliable or useless. It blocks clear thinking and calmness, two elements needed in a crisis.

This sketch points to why fear has become exaggerated, but the deeper question is what made us prey to fear in the first place. The Vedic tradition holds that fear is mind-made. Fear arose, according to this teaching, as the result of a chain of interconnected mistakes known in Sanskrit as *kleshas*. The first and primary mistake is the delusion that the impermanent world of appearances is reality. This leads to identifying yourself with the ego and the body. What you identify with, you become attached to, and, inevitably, attachment creates its opposite, aversion. The ultimate aversion is losing your life, so fear of death is the end of a chain of mistakes that began with illusion.

If we accept the reality of the five kleshas, which are intellectual mistakes, correcting the mistakes isn't intellectual—otherwise, simply reading about them would break the spell of fear. Only awakening can do that. No thinking is required, no inner healing or investigation of old wounds. The psychological aspect of fear, which is unique to human beings, is overcome by transcending the level where psychological fear occurs. A popular modern saying inspired by Taoist teaching puts it this way: *If you are depressed, you are living in the past. If you are anxious, you are living in the future. If you are at peace, you are living in the present.*

This teaching marks out a clear path to ending the grip of fear, but not a simple one. Living in the present has become as complicated as the issue of fear itself; whole books are devoted to it. A lot of underbrush is cleared away by experiencing that simple awareness is always in the present. Getting thrown out of the present happens psychologically. We get distracted, agitated, overwhelmed, numb, too depressed or anxious to rise above the symptoms of depression and anxiety.

Under those conditions, the wisest advice about mindfulness, meditation, contemplation, inner reflection, and Yoga can't sink in. The mind is overcome by the psyche. It is only honest to say that teachings about the source, pure consciousness, and our true nature will also be lost. But one thing can't be lost because our existence depends upon it: simple awareness. Simple awareness is that state of a mind that is calm, balanced, relaxed, and alert. In a hectic world, this can seem like a goal when in reality it is a starting point.

Fear isn't normal, no matter how adjusted we become to living with looming threats and disasters. As J. Krishnamurti bluntly declared, "It is no measure of health to be well-adjusted to a profoundly sick society." Simple awareness doesn't need to be lectured to, because it has no content. Thinking, along with worry, anxiety, dread, and every other manifestation of fear, comes later. On its own, simple awareness looks on life with openness in the moment, nothing more or less.

Access to simple awareness is natural, and you can be in simple awareness by sitting quietly with eyes closed, breathing normally, and placing your attention in the center of your chest. The trick is when to do this. The right time is at the pivot point when you sense a distracted, worried, or stressful state about to emerge but not yet present. Once you pass the pivot point, the decision is made for you—the unwanted response takes charge. Learning to recognize the pivot point is like a mother hearing the first whimper of a baby and knowing that she needs to offer comfort before full-blown distress erupts. You can take the same attitude with your psyche.

The pivot point offers a moment of awareness that is clear and present, like awakening in miniature, so to speak. The habit of being alert to your state of awareness needs to replace the habit of pushing away early warnings or waiting until full-blown anxiety is let loose. Nothing is more important than taking back your power to decide—you put fear on notice that it is no longer free to roam your mind.

Finding Your Wisdom

DEFEATING FEAR

FEAR IS ALMOST IMPOSSIBLE TO DEFEAT ONCE IT TAKES hold. As evidence of this, consider that modern medicine has found no cure for even mild to moderate anxiety. The best that medicine can do is to prescribe tranquilizers, which alleviate symptoms, yet once the patient stops taking the drug, anxiety returns, showing that it was only being masked. Since no historical period has been without its terrors, anxiety seems like a built-in response to threats from the outside world.

In spiritual terms, a different explanation is offered, that fear is inevitable in the state of separation. It is a symptom, not something we need or an automatic response to threats. The awakened life is fearless. On the path to awakening, you can take advantage of the lesson that fear isn't necessary. There are already instances where people act fearlessly, for example, the way firefighters confront a blaze, rather than running away from it or reacting with panic.

Trying to defeat fear after it springs up doesn't work, and defending yourself against fear is generally just as futile. A defense implies a threat; the two go together. The stronger your defenses, the stronger the threat level you are defending against. The practical reasons for installing an alarm system in your home aren't the same as feeling threatened by burglars. The goal should be to do what is needed while remaining unthreatened.

Once you are unthreatened, fear is powerless to gain even a

toehold; this is the opposite of the way that worry and anxiety preoccupy the minds of countless people. Feeling unthreatened is the same as feeling safe, which comes naturally once you apply yourself to dismantling its opposite, feeling unsafe. The project can't take place at the level of the ego, because by its nature "I" is alone, isolated, separate, and therefore insecure. Feeling insecure and feeling safe don't go together.

Feeling safe occurs automatically when you experience your deeper awareness, so your main goal should be to remove the obstacles that block access to deeper awareness. To begin with, come to terms with the widespread belief that Nature is dangerous, catastrophe looms, and therefore the world is a dangerous place. Those beliefs, like all beliefs, are relative. You can attach yourself to any belief, however dire, and the result is self-victimization. Looking the facts squarely in the face doesn't need to have psychological repercussions. Feeling depressed and anxious about climate change, for example, places a distance between you and creative solutions to climate change.

Emotions are dealt with in the branch or limb, or in Yoga known as *Niyama,* which in modern terms is about emotional intelligence. The principal insight from Niyama is that emotions are an organized part of human consciousness that constitute our emotional body. By nature, emotions are aligned with the source. They aren't our enemy, not until they become distorted and thrown out of balance by the mind's interference.

Fear is just such a distortion, which means that it can't be aligned with a healthy emotional body. Your emotional body is composed of awareness, which has a natural ability to heal and rebalance. Knowing this is the foundation of emotional intelligence. A statement as basic as "I feel anxious" combines two aspects of Maya, the insecure ego and a distorted emotion.

Here are six principles to guide you through the process of removing the obstacles posed by fear and anxiety:

- Commit to not complaining, criticizing, or playing the victim.
- Imagine a creative, positive future for yourself.
- Don't regret the past. It no longer exists.
- Be present in every situation as it occurs.
- Be independent of other people's criticism or approval.
- Be responsive to feedback.

You can even turn the six principles into questions posed to yourself.

- Am I complaining, criticizing, or playing the victim?
- Do I see my future in a creative, positive way?
- Am I pointlessly reliving the past?
- Do I see what's going on right now?
- Am I afraid of someone else's criticism or craving their approval?
- Am I listening to what other people are trying to tell me?

These are not mysterious or metaphysical questions. You can pause to ask them anytime you want. Just know that your true nature is safe and secure, while fear is an emotional distortion that can be overcome.

Epilogue

The Lama in My Bedroom

THIS BOOK WAS BASED ON A SINGLE IDEA, THAT A HIDDEN reality beckons behind the illusion of Maya. But it wouldn't be complete without the story of a singular experience, one that took me to the threshold of the waking dream we collectively share.

The story begins with the appearance of a saint in my bedroom. Being interested in higher consciousness doesn't mean that you delve into the so-called supernatural. That changed with a mysterious figure, a saint from the Himalayas, who defied anything I ever expected. *Saint* is a term loosely applied in India to holy men.

This saint from the Himalayas was known in the local region as Lama Sir. The *sir* was a sign of respect shown to a venerable lama, or monk, by inhabitants of the fractious border region between India, China, and Chinese-occupied Tibet. How I came to be connected with Lama Sir still baffles me, and the fact that he started to appear at night in my bedroom in New York City remains impossible to explain by rational means.

I have an Indian friend I'll call K., a television producer who set out to make a documentary about Lama Sir when the monk turned ninety-seven. In his younger years, Lama Sir had been the tutor of the Dalai Lama. K.'s documentary was a go until Lama Sir abruptly decided that he didn't want to be famous, but he and K. remained friends, and as far as anyone knew, Lama Sir had no other outside friends. He lived in solitude in a remote monastery perched precariously on a towering vertical rock face; the site could be accessed only by traversing an 18,000-foot pass (more than 10,000 feet higher than

Aspen, Colorado). Lama Sir encountered other people only if he trekked to visit other monasteries or on the monthly occasions when he went to the nearest border village for provisions.

K. found himself meeting up with Lama Sir almost ten years later, when the monk was 106. For some reason, K. brought up my name. Lama Sir brightened, and he sent some religious talismans or amulets for me and a coral necklace for my wife, Rita. These gifts were duly mailed, along with Lama Sir's words that the talismans aided a seeker on the path to enlightenment and that the necklace was protection for Rita's health.

That night I began to dream about Lama Sir—I recognized him from a photo taken when he was eighty-nine. He said nothing in the dream, but he pointed in several directions. This started a series of dreams in which I saw him, and vaguely, in the way dream images cannot be pinned down, I realized that Lama Sir, a Tibetan Buddhist, was pointing to the various lokas, or worlds, that I knew from The Tibetan Book of Living and Dying.

One night while dreaming, I had the impulse to open my eyes, and when I did, Lama Sir was standing in the room as a three-dimensional apparition. States of awareness blur into each other. In a sleep laboratory, I might have been having a lucid dream, the kind that feels so real it cannot be distinguished from the waking state. I didn't make any speculations of that kind. I felt awake, and Lama Sir was silently standing there.

The fact that this became a nightly event felt like a benediction but also like an uncanny phenomenon. In many Indigenous cultures, the following experiences would be considered uncanny: seeing your double, inanimate objects coming to life, and thoughts appearing to affect the real world. In a religious context, miracles are uncanny. To the modern secular mind, such experiences are viewed skeptically, but moments of awe and wonder also qualify as uncanny, and so do the kind of peak experiences that change lives in a blazing "aha!"

On the scale of uncanniness, Lama Sir appearing in my bedroom topped the charts. I recounted my experiences to K., who has official connections in India, and he proposed taking me to meet Lama Sir in person.

I agreed and made travel arrangements, but on the designated day the weather in the mountains was miserable. Riding in jeeps with a military escort, we ran into sleet and snow on the pass, and when we arrived at the border encampment, the mood was depressing. Young border police were bored out of their skulls patrolling a godforsaken region perpetually in dispute between India, China, and Tibet.

K. walked up with more bad news. Lama Sir's monastery was closed off by the weather, and we wouldn't be seeing him. At that moment, I heard the lama's voice in my ear, his English accented in the way peculiar to this region of northern India. "You are surrounded by too much knowledge," the voice said. "It is blocking your wisdom." The voice was as distinct as the people talking around me.

That was the end and yet the beginning. Lama Sir never re-appeared after that, in my dreams or in any other manifestation. I received news months later that he died at the reputed age of 106.

My experience reinforced my long-held conviction that reality urgently needs rescuing. Too many problems face humanity that only the presence of awakened people can solve. The rescue operation is only complete when reality matches the truth of who we really are and why we are here. In this book, I've presented a path to awakening that everyone can follow—I hope you are intrigued.

Appendix

The Chopra Well-Being Index

. . .

AWAKENING HAS BEEN IN THE RELIGIOUS AND SPIRITUAL domain for so many centuries that it's a challenge to bring it into the modern secular world. But that's a necessary step. In today's landscape, a spiritual path must be a practical path, with measurable markers of progress.

The most basic measure of progress is a person's overall well-being. Awakening happens in consciousness, but the ramifications extend to every aspect of a person's life. The Chopra Well-Being Index is comprehensive, going beyond mind and body to include relationships, purpose, and spirit.

The CWI was developed over the years at the Chopra Center for Well-Being in Carlsbad, California, in consultation with staff, meditation teachers, attending physicians, and experience with thousands of patients. The Index is based on self-assessment. It can give you a clear picture of where you stand now, but there is a larger purpose in mind. I urge you to do more than one self-assessment. The first one will be now, before you commit yourself to the path of awakening. The second one can be anytime in the future when enough time has elapsed for your journey to yield results.

There is no set timetable. Each person will sense when the time is right for themselves. Paying attention is the key to the process of awakening, as outlined in this book. If you keep on paying attention, you can return to assess your progress in years to come—I warmly urge you to. Full awakening is a global event in the mind; you find that you are never unaware. Short of that goal, however, awareness becomes subtler and deeper with every step along the path. The results will show up each time you reassess your overall well-being. The CWI has been statistically validated to give you confidence in its findings, but in the end, you are both the witness and the protagonist of your journey. This assessment is offered simply as a useful tool, not a replacement for your own inner knowing.

DIRECTIONS

There are 10 questions in each section. Circle the number that applies to Excellent, Good, Fair, and Poor for each section. Take all the time you need, and feel free to change any of your answers if you have second thoughts.

BODY

Answer the following questions as they apply OVER THE LAST SIX MONTHS.

1.   My general physical health has been

Excellent 10 points
Good 7 points
Fair 4 points
Poor 2 points

YOUR SCORE _____ POINTS

2.   How many prescription drugs do you take?

None—Excellent 10 points
1—Good 7 points
2 or 3—Fair 4 points
4 or more—Poor 2 points

YOUR SCORE _____ POINTS

3. How close are you to your ideal weight (measured around age 20 for most people)?

> No change, weigh the same or less—
> Excellent 10 points
> Gained 5–10 pounds—Good 7 points
> Gained no more than 20 percent of ideal weight
> (approximately 3 pounds for every 20 pounds)—
> Fair 4 points
> Consider myself very overweight/obese—
> Poor 2 points

YOUR SCORE _____ **POINTS**

4. Compared to my peak energy earlier in life, my present energy is

> Excellent 10 points
> Good 7 points
> Fair 4 points
> Poor 2 points

YOUR SCORE _____ **POINTS**

5. My blood pressure is

> Excellent 10 points
> Good 7 points
> Fair 4 points
> Poor 2 points

YOUR SCORE _____ **POINTS**

6. My weekly physical activity includes

> Regular strenuous exercise or Yoga—
> Excellent 10 points
> Regular light exercise—Good 7 points

Getting up and moving around during the day—
   Fair 4 points
Sedentary lifestyle—Poor 2 points

YOUR SCORE _____ POINTS

7. Knowing what I know about eating a healthy diet, I'd rate my current dietary lifestyle as

Excellent 10 points
Good 7 points
Fair 4 points
Poor 2 points

YOUR SCORE _____ POINTS

8. The number of sick days I had to take in the last six months (either from work or from regular activity) is

1 or none—Excellent 10 points
2–4 days—Good 7 points
5–7 days—Fair 4 points
More than 7 days—Poor 2 points

YOUR SCORE _____ POINTS

9. Compared with the healthiest people I know, I consider my health status

Excellent 10 points
Good 7 points
Fair 4 points
Poor 2 points

YOUR SCORE _____ POINTS

10. Has anyone in your immediate family, or any close relatives, died of heart attack, stroke, diabetes, or cancer before age 65?

1 or none—Excellent 10 points
2 people—Good 7 points

3 people—Fair 4 points
More than 3 people—Poor 2 points

YOUR SCORE _____ **POINTS**

TOTAL BODY SCORE _____ **points**

·

MIND

Answer the following questions OVER THE LAST MONTH.

1. **My general mood has been**

   Excellent 10 points
   Good 7 points
   Fair 4 points
   Poor 2 points

   YOUR SCORE _____ **POINTS**

2. **Do you feel depressed about how your life is going?**

   Not at all—Excellent 10 points
   A few times, but it soon passes—Good 7 points
   Fairly often or for more than a few days—Fair 4 points
   Depressed more than half the time—Poor 2 points

   YOUR SCORE _____ **POINTS**

3. **How stressed do you feel?**

   Relaxed and unstressed—Excellent 10 points
   Under pressure, but I feel in control of it—
       Good 7 points
   I feel stressed too often—Fair 4 points
   Stress has gotten the upper hand in my life—
       Poor 2 points

   YOUR SCORE _____ **POINTS**

4. **How would you rate your level of anxiety and worry?**

    Excellent 10 points
    Good 7 points
    Fair 4 points
    Poor 2 points

YOUR SCORE _____ POINTS

5. **Do you feel the need for psychotherapy, tranquilizers, or antidepressants?**

    No, and never have—Excellent 10 points
    Not now, but it might help—Good 7 points
    Currently in therapy or taking tranquilizers or
        antidepressants—Fair 4 points
    Dependent on therapy, tranquilizers, or
        antidepressants—Poor 2 points

YOUR SCORE _____ POINTS

6. **How do you feel about your personal finances?**

    Excellent 10 points
    Good 7 points
    Fair 4 points
    Poor 2 points

YOUR SCORE _____ POINTS

7. **How would you rate your sense of self-worth?**

    Excellent 10 points
    Good 7 points
    Fair 4 points
    Poor 2 points

YOUR SCORE _____ POINTS

8. Do you have deep regrets, wounds from your past, guilt, or self-judgment?

> No, or rarely—Excellent 10 points
> Not really—Good 7 points
> About the same as other people—Fair 4 points
> More than my share—Poor 2 points

YOUR SCORE _____ POINTS

9. How well do you focus and pay attention?

> Very sharply focused and organized—
> Excellent 10 points
> Good focus anytime I want to—Good 7 points
> Many distractions (smartphone, social media,
> video games)—Fair 4 points
> I have a hard time focusing and getting things done—
> Poor 2 points

YOUR SCORE _____ POINTS

10. How do you feel about growing older?

> Excellent 10 points
> Good 7 points
> Fair 4 points
> Poor 2 points

YOUR SCORE _____ POINTS

TOTAL MIND SCORE _____ points

•

RELATIONSHIPS

Note: Answer the following questions as they relate to your whole range of close relationships with your spouse/partner, family, friends, and close co-workers OVER THE LAST THREE MONTHS.

I.   How happy are you when it comes to your personal relationships?

>   Very happy—10 points
>   Happy with no serious exceptions—7 points
>   Pretty happy, but with some exceptions—4 points
>   Some ups, some downs, but they aren't my fault—
>   2 points

YOUR SCORE _____ **POINTS**

2.   Have you ever been, or are you now, deeply in love?

>   I am right now—10 points
>   Yes, in the past, and it was a very meaningful
>   experience—7 points
>   Yes, but it is mostly a memory now—4 points
>   Not really—2 points

YOUR SCORE _____ **POINTS**

3.   What does a good relationship mean to you?

>   A high level of love, trust, respect, and sharing—
>   10 points
>   Being important in each other's lives, looking out for
>   each other, feeling close—7 points
>   A nice level of affection, compatibility, and
>   togetherness—4 points
>   Getting along, having a good time, not butting in or
>   causing problems—2 points

YOUR SCORE _____ **POINTS**

4. **Can you rely on your relationship for emotional support and encouragement?**

> Yes, definitely. It's a strong part of my close relationships—10 points
>
> Yes, but things haven't been tested in a crisis— 7 points
>
> It's not something that comes up very often, but each of us supports the other—4 points
>
> I look out for myself. It's no one else's business— 2 points

YOUR SCORE _____ POINTS

5. **What do you contribute to your relationships?**

> I am deeply involved. I care for others almost as much as I care for myself—10 points
>
> I am always there to give and support— 7 points
>
> I can be counted on. I am reliable and helpful— 4 points
>
> I give and take about equally—2 points

YOUR SCORE _____ POINTS

6. **What do you receive from your relationships?**

> We are equals in every important way, and we grow together—10 points
>
> I get love, support, and a good emotional connection—7 points
>
> I get a nice sense of closeness, sharing, and good companionship—4 points
>
> I don't ask a lot, and that's about what I get in return—2 points

YOUR SCORE _____ POINTS

7.   If something goes wrong, do you resent or forgive?

> I have no lingering resentments. I forgive easily—
>   10 points
> Some things I might resent, but I always try to forgive,
>   even when it is difficult—7 points
> I'm fair, but some things you can't forgive—
>   4 points
> I have to confess, I hold grudges a long time—
>   2 points

YOUR SCORE ___ POINTS

8.   How are you with the four A's: attention, appreciation, affection, and acceptance?

> Excellent 10 points
> Good 7 points
> Fair 4 points
> Poor 2 points

YOUR SCORE _____ POINTS

9.   How would you rate your family life overall?

> Excellent 10 points
> Good 7 points
> Fair 4 points
> Poor 2 points

YOUR SCORE _____ POINTS

10.   When disagreements arise, how do you deal with them?

> I actively seek a solution and empathize with the other
>   person—10 points
> I discuss the disagreement openly and honestly, but I
>   also stick to my guns—7 points

I tend to avoid any confrontation and hope things work
out on their own—4 points

I hold to my position, because I'm usually right—
2 points

YOUR SCORE _____ **POINTS**

TOTAL RELATIONSHIPS SCORE _____ **points**

•

PURPOSE

Answer the following questions as they relate to you IN THE
PRESENT.

1.   Do you feel that you are leading a meaningful life?

Definitely, meaningful in the highest way—10 points
Yes, I have a solid sense of purpose—7 points
Pretty meaningful most of the time—4 points
Things feel pretty meaningless most days—2 points

YOUR SCORE _____ **POINTS**

2.   Do you feel you are here to serve others (leaving aside family)?

Definitely, I am very dedicated to service—10 points
Yes, I set aside time for service activity—7 points
I help out people close to me when I can—4 points
I don't really think in terms of service—2 points

YOUR SCORE _____ **POINTS**

3.   How grateful are you for the life you lead?

Very grateful, it is a major focus every day—10 points
Consistently grateful when I happen to think about
it—7 points

I am generally grateful if someone asks me—4 points

I don't have much to be grateful for—2 points

YOUR SCORE _____ POINTS

4. **Would you say your life is guided by a higher purpose?**

Yes, definitely. It is the focus of my life—10 points

Yes, I aim to be a better person whenever I can—
7 points

I am not guided, but I follow the beliefs and morality
I was brought up with—4 points

No, I am preoccupied with surviving and getting
ahead—2 points

YOUR SCORE _____ POINTS

5. **Looking back, have inspiring role models played a part in your life?**

Yes, definitely. Without them, I wouldn't be who I am
today—10 points

Yes, but mostly in my family—7 points

I have heroes, but I didn't model my life on them—
4 points

I took care of myself without needing a role model—
2 points

YOUR SCORE _____ POINTS

6. **How do you affect the people around you?**

I am a leader, role model, or inspiration—10 points

I have often been told I am a positive influence—
7 points

I have a good effect on family and friends—4 points

It's not something I really think about—2 points

YOUR SCORE _____ POINTS

7. What is the effect of the work you do? (If retired, a student, or a stay-at-home parent, think of your main daily activity.)

> My work changes people's lives or improves the
> world—10 points
> My work benefits more than me and my family—
> 7 points
> My work benefits me and my family—
> 4 points
> My job is just a job—2 points

YOUR SCORE _____ POINTS

8. How have your biggest dreams turned out?

> Excellent 10 points
> Good 7 points
> Fair 4 points
> Poor 2 points

YOUR SCORE _____ POINTS

9. Looking back, how much of your life would you change?

> Nothing—10 points
> Very little—7 points
> One or two important things that went wrong—
> 4 points
> I'd change a lot—2 points

YOUR SCORE _____ POINTS

10. Looking back, do you think things happened to you for a reason?

> Yes, definitely. Everything happened to help me in
> some way—10 points
> Yes, although I can't tell you why—7 points

Mostly, there were accidents and wrong turns, too—
4 points

Life is life. Things don't happen for a reason—
2 points

YOUR SCORE _____ POINTS

TOTAL PURPOSE SCORE _____ points

•

SPIRIT

Answer the following questions as they relate to you OVER THE
LAST THREE MONTHS.

1. Looking at my life, the spiritual part is

    The most important—10 points
    Something I value—7 points
    Pretty much the same as always—4 points
    Not something I think about—2 points

    YOUR SCORE _____ POINTS

2. How do you feel about God, a higher power, or cosmic
    consciousness?

    It's a critical part of my life—10 points
    I am definitely a believer—7 points
    Faith and skepticism both cross my mind—4 points
    I am skeptical or don't really care—2 points

    YOUR SCORE _____ POINTS

3. Have you felt what you'd call the presence of spirit?

    Yes, in very important ways—10 points
    I am pretty sure I have—7 points

Maybe or maybe not—4 points

No or don't care—2 points

YOUR SCORE _____ POINTS

4.   How do you feel about the afterlife?

Certain it exists—10 points

More accepting than rejecting—7 points

Hopeful but definitely uncertain—4 points

Skeptical, because there is no evidence for an afterlife—2 points

YOUR SCORE _____ POINTS

5.   Do you believe you have a soul or a higher self?

Absolutely, I have experienced it—10 points

Yes, because I think I've experienced it—7 points

Yes, because of my religion and upbringing—4 points

No, because there is no scientific evidence to support it—2 points

YOUR SCORE _____ POINTS

6.   Is meditation part of your life?

Yes, I consistently meditate every day—10 points

Yes, I meditate fairly regularly—7 points

I only meditate if I feel I really need it—4 points

No, I don't meditate—2 points

YOUR SCORE _____ POINTS

7.   How do you feel about enlightenment, however you define that term?

It is one of my goals in life—10 points

It exists and I have deep respect for it—7 points

It's not something I think about one way or the
　　other—4 points
It doesn't exist or has nothing to do with me—2 points

YOUR SCORE _____ POINTS

8.　How do you relate to the human potential movement, personal
　　evolution, and higher consciousness?

Avidly interested and involved—10 points
This appeals to me, and I have seriously looked into
　　it—7 points
Self-improvement is about as far as I go, here and
　　there—4 points
Don't believe in it or not interested—2 points

YOUR SCORE _____ POINTS

9.　Can you rely on your prayers, wishes, or intentions to come true?

Yes, I depend upon it—10 points
Yes, that has happened quite a few times—7 points
Not really, but I am hopeful—4 points
No or not interested—2 points

YOUR SCORE _____ POINTS

10.　Have you met or do you know someone you admire as highly
　　spiritual?

Yes, and that person is important in my life—10 points
Yes, in passing—7 points
No, but my religion says they exist—4 points
No or don't believe they exist—2 points

YOUR SCORE _____ POINTS

TOTAL SPIRIT SCORE _____ points

·

TOTALS

Body ____ points
Mind ____ points
Relationships ____ points
Purpose _____ points
Spirit ____ points

OVERALL SCORE _____ **points**

·

WHAT DOES YOUR SCORE TELL YOU?

Your scores, both individual and overall, can be assessed to give you valuable information about your state of well-being.

OVERALL SCORE

When you add up the five areas of Body, Mind, Relationships, Purpose, and Spirit, your overall score will be between 100 points and 500 points. The two extremes are not feasible, because no one's life is totally Poor or totally Excellent.

SCORES REALISTICALLY FALL INTO THREE CATEGORIES:

Good to Excellent (350 points or more)

If your score falls into this range, your overall well-being is very secure. It is hard to attain such a high score without having each area be consistently high. Your life is very balanced in all areas, which isn't possible without a strong sense of self-awareness. You lead a conscious lifestyle. Poor decisions and bad lifestyle choices are rare for you, and you know how to correct them, because you feel in general that your life is under your control. You are in a good position to explore higher consciousness, and in all probability you have undertaken a spiritual journey of some kind. You are well on the path, whether you use that term or not.

Fair to Good (250–350 points)

If your score falls into this category, you have a good sense of well-being, but beyond that, it is hard to generalize. The five areas of your life—body, mind, relationships, purpose, and spirit—could score about the same, but that isn't likely. Probably you have a mixture of stronger and weaker areas. In other words, your life is inconsistent. You feel good about one or more areas but not so good about others. Perhaps you have good physical health but a rocky or routine relationship and not much of a spiritual life—any combination is possible—which is why, for you, the overall score doesn't say much. Your individual scores tell you where you need to pay the most attention.

Poor to Fair (below 250 points)

If your score falls into this category, you are probably struggling. Instead of thinking about your well-being, you are preoccupied with staying afloat, and sometimes you wonder if you are even getting anywhere in your life. This isn't the same as feeling miserable. You might look in the mirror and find nothing particularly different from what you are used to, or what your family background has taught you to expect from life. If your score is closer to the upper end (200 points or higher), you might think that your life is no worse than the next person's.

But what is more likely is that you have had some serious setbacks. Many scenarios are possible, including a bad divorce, losing your job, or contracting a life-threatening disorder. The import is basically the same, however: Your well-being isn't what it should be and may even be declining over time. Even your average expectations may have been disappointed.

INDIVIDUAL SCORES

For each area, your score will be between 20 points and 100 points. However, the two extremes aren't really feasible. Twenty points would mean a rating of Poor on every question; 100 points would mean a rating of Excellent on every question.

As with your overall score, individual scores realistically fall into three categories:

Good to Excellent (70 points or more)

If your score falls into this category, you enjoy a superior state of well-being, and it would be fair to say that you are thriving. Your beliefs, choices, habits, lifestyle, and self-worth are high. You might or might not be favored by education, privilege, or social standing. Those factors are less important than your self-awareness. For you, the horizon of the future is promising. Your path is to go beyond your current limitations and explore more possibilities in life.

Fair to Good (50–70 points)

If your score falls into this category, your well-being is more or less the norm. You are not simply surviving, but you are not thriving, either. Wellness and self-care may not figure very much in your daily life, probably because you haven't seriously considered them or you take a fairly casual approach to them. The good news is that you are in a position to make big leaps in your well-being. All it takes is paying more attention to your happiness and raising your expectations. You sense your unfulfilled potential; now you need to act on it. Better lifestyle choices, beliefs, and habits are at hand if you reach out for them.

Poor to Fair (below 50 points)

If your score falls into this category, your well-being is compromised. You probably feel discouraged or under considerable stress much of the time. Just surviving and getting along has been your main concern. If you fall into the higher end of this category (40 points or more), you might be getting along about as well as the people you know. But you need to raise your expectations quite a lot. You are selling yourself short. Life has much more to offer, but something fairly major is holding you back. In each area where your score is low, sit down and list the reason you're doing only Fair to Poor. Start with what you can begin to improve upon right now. A stronger sense of self needs to become a primary goal. You deserve a higher state of well-being, which begins only when you think you deserve it. You do, most certainly. Now is the time to value yourself more so that you can gain control of your life.

MOVING FORWARD

Now that you have answered the Index questions, look back at how your Self-Assessment matches your expectations beforehand.

- If your Self-Assessment closely matches your Index score, you know yourself well in that area, whether it is mind, body, relationships, purpose, or spirit. You are in a good position to expand your awareness and increase your well-being in the future.
- If your Self-Assessment is significantly higher than your

Index score, you need to be more realistic about the area in question. Maybe you are just optimistic, but there is probably some other element at work: denial, hopeful or wishful thinking, or not wanting to see things clearly. It is time to come back down to Earth and make an effort to improve this area (or areas) of your life. It is time to lead a life that actually matches your high expectations.

- If your Self-Assessment is significantly lower than your Index score, you probably feel conflicted. You sell yourself short or don't want to be self-centered. In any case, your baseline is too low. Your life is objectively going better than you assume. In the future your aim should be to develop a secure sense of self that matches how well you are actually doing in life. It is time to raise your expectations.

Your overall and individual scores aren't telling you anything you don't already know. But by having an objective score, you have a baseline for future comparison. There are many ways to improve your well-being, as given in articles, books, and meditations I've written. These methods work; thousands of people have benefited from them over many years. The important thing is for you to give yourself a chance to be happier, healthier, and living a better life. From that intention, all progress grows.

One obstacle might be that you find it easy to let weaker areas slide because you feel good about other areas. This is only natural. In modern society the strongest emphasis is placed on physical well-being first, relationships second, and mental well-being third, with little focus on spiritual life and purpose beyond the basics. If your sense of self follows the normal pattern, your focus will be to stay healthy, be in a solid relationship, and avoid depression and anxiety.

The Chopra Well-Being Index can expand your horizons considerably. Sit down and look closely at the area where you scored lowest. You might get some clues from the other answers, but even without this, consider how to change your attitude, beliefs, and choices when it comes to a question where you scored low.

Acknowledgments

Probably more than any of my books, this one owes its final shape to two people who guided and advised me along the way. Gary Jansen, my invaluable editor for many years, was the first to see that the focus should be spiritual awakening. For that, along with all your other contributions and abiding friendship, heartfelt thanks.

This was my first book working with executive editor Matthew Benjamin, and it was eye-opening to experience the care and detail of his sympathetic attention as the manuscript unfolded. Thanks especially for seeing how much would be added by devoting a section to the Chopra Well-Being Index.

It's a fortunate writer who can look back on even a single book that might stand as a legacy, but the legacy that sustains me here and now is my beloved family. My wife, Rita, our children, Gotham and Mallika, and now the grandchildren represent a shared journey that began more than fifty years ago when I fell in love with Rita. Deep down, no time has passed at all.

Index

ABOUT THE AUTHOR

DEEPAK CHOPRA, MD, founder of the Chopra Foundation and Chopra Global, is a world-renowned pioneer in integrative medicine and personal transformation. He is also the founder of DigitalDeepak.ai, a groundbreaking initiative utilizing advanced AI technology to communicate his timeless wisdom worldwide, helping and guiding individuals on their path to well-being and personal growth. Chopra is the author of more than ninety books, including numerous *New York Times* bestsellers. *Time* magazine has described Dr. Chopra as "one of the top 100 heroes and icons of the century."